BLOSSOMS

from the

FLOWERY KINGDOM

Yours sincerely,
Bessie Cordell

BLOSSOMS
from the
FLOWERY KINGDOM
by
BESSIE CORDELL
Missionary of United Missionary Society
Author of "Precious Pearl"

First printing, 1944
Second printing, 1946
Third printing, 1949

PRINTED IN U. S. A. BY *Light and Life Press*, WINONA LAKE, INDIANA

TABLE OF CONTENTS

LIST OF ILLUSTRATIONS

INTRODUCTION

CHINA! LAND OF ANTIQUITY. We think of other nations in terms of decades or centuries, but of China in terms of millenniums.

To this enchanting land, which calls itself the Flowery Kingdom, messengers of the Cross have gone forth. From the days of the pioneer missionaries in the early part of the 19th century the work of God has steadily advanced. Before the outbreak of war between China and Japan in 1937, there were approximately a half million Christians in China. During the past few years that number has more than doubled.

During her last term of service as a missionary in Shantung Province in North China, Miss Cordell shared with the Chinese the dangers and privations caused by the war. She bravely remained alone in her station during a period when opposing forces were struggling for the possession of that area.

Out of the background of her own personal experience, an intimate knowledge of conditions and a personal acquaintanceship with the persons about whom she writes, she here sets forth in her own attractive style an account of the spiritual experiences and growth of a number of her Chinese Christian friends and co-workers.

We believe this little volume, "Blossoms from the Flowery Kingdom," will be a source of inspiration and great spiritual blessing to many.

GEORGE R. WARNER

T HE FIRST five or six months of her life, Tiny lay in a dark inner room on a hard brick bed. The walls of the room were made of mud. A hole cut through the partition connected this gloomy little room with the outer one which was less dismal, because there was a door opening into a small courtyard. The neighboring houses were so close to this one that only the midday sun could brighten and warm the humble home.

No one arose early during the cold winter days, for it was the custom to eat two meals each day even during the good years. By the time the morning work was finished, the sun was high in the sky. The courtyard was then warm enough for the women to sit on a straw mat with their work spread out before them.

When Tiny had slept until she could sleep no longer, she would stretch her bare little arms and yawn softly. She could not play with her toes, for she was wearing a dust bag to keep her warm and to save her mother work, but she often put her skinny fist into her mouth. She frequently rolled her head from side to side while her bright eyes slowly searched for the mellow light which shone through the paper window high above her head. Her mother made her a pretty little cap such as babies wear all the time when they are infants. She did this by taking a narrow strip of red cloth, long enough to go around the child's head after the two ends were sewed together. Then she gathered the cloth on top, leaving a large, round hole in the middle which showed the baby's soft black hair.

As Tiny grew older, she was no longer content to stay in a room all by herself. She kicked and screamed at the top of her voice, so her mother said that she was old enough to get up. Since the dust bag was too heavy and clumsy to be carried about, Tiny was taken out of it during the daytime and carried next to her mother's warm skin. She was securely fastened by a strong girdle tied around her mother's waist.

The mother hurrying here and there, busy with her many duties, carried the babe as she worked. She lifted the wooden lid from the iron kettle and dipped the hot millet porridge into coarse earthen bowls for her husband and his parents. She had already put the steamed bread and salted garlic on the table. Bringing a pair of chopsticks she placed them beside each of the bowls and stood ready to serve the others while they ate noisily and quickly. When they had eaten until they were full, Tiny's mother scraped the food loose from the bottom and sides of the cauldron and added some water to it. This was her portion, and it would be the portion of her little girl.

Tiny loved to snatch at her mother's thread when she tried to spin, or even when she sewed. As the feeble arms grew stronger, the mother was hindered in her work. Sometimes Grandfather would fold the little girl in the front of his long gown and tie the strong girdle around his waist.

There were times when the father liked to carry the babe

in his bosom when he went to the shops to buy matches or tea leaves. He felt rather embarrassed that his first born was not a boy, but his heart softened toward the baby as she cuddled her warm, supple body against his firm, hard flesh. How small and soft she was!

Tiny was more intelligent than her father expected a girl to be. Why, she noticed things on the street just like a baby boy would have done! One day when he was quite pleased with the little one, he fumbled in his girdle until he found a copper which he gave to a passing vendor for a stick of red haws dipped in sugar. Of course, the baby could not eat the haws but she loved to play with them, and she could taste the sweetness as she put the stick into her mouth.

Adverse circumstances came to this happy family, and their poverty grew with the passing of the days. Tiny was always hungry and often fretted because she wanted something to eat. The tired mother many times took some of the dark bread which was her own portion and chewed it as fine as she could. Then she would put her lips up close to the wide open ones of the child and fill her mouth, even as a mother bird feeds her young.

A few days after the grandmother died, a new bride was brought to the home to take her place. Although she was younger than Tiny's father and mother, filial obedience demanded that they treat her as an elder and always address her as "mother." To be sure, she was not a handsome girl or her parents would never have married her to a man so much older, especially when they received only a paltry dowry for her.

Grandma was cross and grumbled all the time because the home was so poor. She scolded Tiny's mother about many things, and complained because the food was not better. The mother was very patient and taught her little one that she must be patient too. The child soon learned that girls could not eat the same kind of food as boys, for boys are permitted to eat with their elders. Not once did the mother complain, but she secretly longed for a son. She hoped that she might be a mother-in-law herself some day, and thus receive the honor due her.

Tiny would stand leaning against her mother's knee and tugging at her breast, even when the flabby flesh would scarcely yield any food. About that time a son was born to the grandmother. There being more nourishment than the little uncle needed, he shared with Tiny until he became big and strong enough to push her away.

Mother had two married sisters who were older than herself. Their homes were not as poor, and they enjoyed Tiny's childish prattle, for neither of them had a child of her own. Tiny's mother often led her wee daughter to the home of first one aunt and then the other. When she grew too homesick for her mother, she was taken back to her own home. After some days had passed, and the child again cried because she was so hungry, her mother would take her back to the home of one of the aunts.

One day when hunger pangs were gnawing at the little one's stomach and her puny legs were too weak to carry her farther, she lay down in the dusty road and wailed in misery. The mother plucked an ear of unripe corn from a field by

4

the road side, removed the green husk, and gave it to her child. After she had eaten two or three ears of the corn, the pain in her stomach ceased and added strength began to come into the small, bony legs. She dragged wearily on beside

Wash Day

her mother until they reached the home of her mother's eldest sister once more.

Of course, Tiny's feet had to be bound or no man would ever want her for a wife. Golden-lily feet could be obtained only at a price—suffering. Every little girl knew that she must endure pain if she would have small feet when she grew old enough for marriage. She knew, too, that the smaller her feet, the better her offers of marriage were likely to be. The correct length of a bound foot was considered to be four inches. Tiny often sat on the brick bed, holding her small, aching feet. When the pain was too great, she would wipe her ragged sleeve furtively across her blinking eyes, but never once did she ask her mother to loosen the long blue strips of home-spun cloth which tightly bound her crippled feet. She even dreamed of dainty shoes that she would make of bright scraps of satin when she sometime married a rich official. She liked to think of the good food and beautiful clothes that might some day be hers. Gladly she bore the pain and discomfort because she did not want to have big feet.

One day a red envelope was brought to Tiny's home. Inside the envelope was a red slip of paper, and on this paper was written the name of her future husband. Her parents did not reveal their plans to her until they told her that she was engaged.

A few months later, the middle-man brought another red paper, and this one announced the date for the wedding. The groom's family sent some pretty flowered cloth for quilts and cloth for the wedding garments, and they sent a few toilet articles and hair ornaments such as brides wore.

Tiny was very busy making everything by hand. As she twisted small bias strings of cloth to make loops and buttons for her new jacket, she wondered what her new home would be like. She would ask herself, "Can I be patient when my mother-in-law scolds me? Will my husband be satisfied with me? What shall I do if he is cross and beats me?"

Tiny was married when she was sixteen. Her husband was an industrious young man. He was employed to run errands and sweep the courtyards at the county magistrate's and was paid well for his work. They found a house closer to his work, and another son took care of the aged parents. There was enough food and clothing to keep them in comfort, even after their three sons were born. Tiny was content.

When the magistrate was moved, Mr. T'u lost his position and could find no work anywhere. Tiny sought for something to do and worked at the most menial tasks. She washed for other people, taking the clothes to the pond where she would squat on her small feet, while she dipped the dirty garments into the cold water and tried to wash them clean, without any soap, by rubbing them on the rocks. In the winter her hands were so rough and chapped that blood oozed from the cracks, and she had no ointment to soothe them.

Mr. T'u grew discouraged because he could find nothing to do, for he was not an idle man by nature. To forget his troubles and while away the long hours, he went to the Christian Chapel. In a short time he became a follower of the Jesus teaching.

Mrs. T'u was bitter because she had to work so hard to feed the family, and they never had enough to satisfy their hunger even at that. It displeased her that her husband spent time he could ill afford listening to the foreign devils when he should be searching for something to do.

Mr. T'u told his wife how kind the missionaries were, and

he tried to tell her about the peace that had come to his own heart. He asked her to listen while he sang a hymn which he had just learned. This angered Mrs. T'u, and she would not listen. She went to a neighbor's home rather than hear the song. For two years things went on this way.

Mr. T'u pleaded with his wife to go to the mission and hear for herself. One Sunday a neighbor woman invited Mrs. T'u to go with her to the meeting. She went. She listened very attentively to the first message she had ever heard and went into the inquirer's room at the close of the service. From that day she never wanted to miss a single Sunday.

Mr. T'u developed a hard cough, and with the coming of bitter, wintry days he grew worse. His thin body shivered in his patched, ragged clothes, and his face was drawn and sallow. Since Mrs. T'u could not earn enough money to feed so many mouths and pay the house rent, they moved into a haunted house and did not pay rent.

When little money could be obtained by working for others, Mrs. T'u and the children went out to beg. Mr. T'u became so weak that he could no longer drag himself from his bed. It was evident that he could not last much longer. The burdened wife went to see a prosperous nephew who owned about sixteen acres of land. As the sound of footsteps came through the open door, the nephew's wife looked quickly to see who was coming. When she saw the little woman, she knew why she had come, so bolted the door fast and would not open it.

Heavy-hearted and discouraged, Mrs. T'u slowly returned to her home of poverty. What could she do next? Must she bury her husband without a coffin and let the dogs eat his flesh? A Christian went to see one of the missionaries and put the problem before him. When he returned from his visit, he carried the price of a cheap wood coffin in his hand. An unpainted box was bought immediately and carried into the yard to be ready when needed.

Another friend went to the nephew's home, and since they did not know him or the reason why he came, they listened to his request. He brought back with him enough money for a new padded coat. As soon as the garment could be purchased, they quickly put it on the dying man so that he would not have to be dressed after he was dead.

When he had breathed his last, Tiny straightened his arms and legs and closed his staring, unseeing eyes. Then she covered him with his ragged quilt and went to call the neighbors to help put him into the coffin. Some of the neighbors were angry because she would not have a hole cut through the mud wall, large enough for the big coffin to pass through, rather than have it carried through the front gate where it would be easy for the evil spirits to find other places to abide.

The next morning, some of the Christians came with the evangelist to conduct the funeral. The huge rough box stood on some benches in the little yard where all could see. After the last song was sung, ropes of hemp were put under the coffin and pulled up around the sides. Then the carriers put poles through the ropes and heaved the poles to their shoulders. They carried the corpse to a near-by temple yard and buried it there. Mrs. T'u's sons wore coarse white cloth bands around their sleeves, and patches of the white cloth had been sewed to their shoes. On the way to the grave they prostrated themselves to show their grief, and they wailed at the top of their voices, "Ah, my father! How can we live without your care?"

The smallest child stayed at the house with his mother who watched the home, as it was not proper for her to go to the grave. After the funeral, the owner of the borrowed house demanded that Mrs. T'u vacate it at once. The mother and her boys carried their few belongings to an old temple which was to be their home for the next six months. Two of the boys found places where they could work for their board, and the smallest one died.

A relative opened a hot water shop and needed some one to keep the kettles boiling. They offered to give Mrs. T'u her food in return for her work, but she must work from early morning until late at night with no time off for Sunday meetings.

About this time, a woman was needed to keep the gate in the women's court at the mission. A Christian woman, knowing of Mrs. T'u's difficulties and her desire to follow the Christian doctrine, felt that she would be the very one for the place. She volunteered to call Mrs. T'u to come out for an interview. When the timid woman heard that she was wanted at the mission, her heart was filled with fear.

"I do not dare go out there and see the white woman!" she exclaimed. "What can she want with me? Look at my dirty clothes—they are so ragged that I am not fit to be seen on the street!"

A kind neighbor who had seen the stranger go to the hot water shop dropped in to learn the purpose of the visit. She at once offered the loan of her own coarse blue garment. It was large enough to slip on over Mrs. T'u's soiled one, and it was long enough to cover part of her baggy old trousers. The smoke of the fire was washed from her face, and the wooden comb run through her hair. Then she coiled the hair into a tiny knot at the nape of her neck and stuck a large pin through it, and she was ready to go.

"What can they want of me?" she kept muttering. "I never stole any of their things."

Although assured that this was not why she was sent for, the nearer they came to the mission compound, the harder and faster Mrs. T'u's heart pounded. She kept asking herself, over and over, "How shall I answer if they accuse me of having stolen anything from them?"

Mrs. T'u was very happy in her new position. She was so eager to learn to read the Bible that she wept bitterly because she was more stupid than the rest, but, year after year, she kept at it, until she had memorized many passages. Because she could not learn as easily as the others, she was often asked to care for the children while their mothers were in classes. The children loved her. She kept them amused and playing happily, many times holding a tiny baby in her bosom while entertaining the others.

Her salary was small, but there would have been enough for her to live in comfort had not one of the boys come to beg for her money so often. She did not refuse to help him and often went without food for a day or two at a time while waiting for her next monthly allowance. A few years ago this son died and the other one went north to seek work, so the mother has been free to use her money for herself.

Since Mrs. T'u had known what it was to be hungry most of her life, she gladly shared her food with others. No Christian woman was ever allowed to leave the women's court hungry if it were in Mrs. T'u's power to help her.

Mrs. T'u had been failing in health for sometime, and when our buildings were taken over she sat cross-legged on her k'ang with her head bowed in sorrow. She was so frightened that she did not make any sound when the Japanese sealed the door of her room with her sitting there like a Buddha. When a friend found her thus, with her door pasted shut and stamped with the seal of the Japanese army, she informed the officials, who laughingly removed the seal and let the old lady come out. From that day, Mrs. T'u failed rapidly, and she knew that her time had come to go.

The nephew who refused to help her when her husband was dying, came to see her one day. He brought her ten dollars, although he is not as prosperous as he was when she needed his help so sorely. Mrs. T'u testified again and again that she was ready to go, and she prayed that she might not have to tarry.

A new grave was dug on the mission burying ground one morning. The plain, unvarnished box was brought a few days before, and Mrs. T'u was dressed in her burial clothes. At noon, she went peacefully to be with her Lord.

Conditions hindered our having a funeral such as was due one so old, but that afternoon a few Christians gathered at the door of the women's courtyard for a brief service. Tears came to their eyes as Pastor Wang reminded those present that Mrs. T'u had carried their babies down through the years, making it possible for them to be in the meetings and classes.

For more than twenty-five years, Mrs. T'u has served the mission faithfully and to the very best of her ability. She poured hot water for the women who came to meetings on Sunday and made them feel at home. She is missed by those who have been recipients of her kindness, but we rejoice that she shall never suffer again.

Many have had a more brilliant career than Mrs. T'u. She never led a meeting in her life; she never saw her name in print; she could not write a letter nor read one when it was written; but she served her Lord to the very best of her ability. It can truly be said of her, "She hath done what she could."

FAITHFUL CHANG

J UST TEN LI from the Drum tower at Tungchangfu, in
the village of Shih Li Ying, lived an old couple with their
son and his wife and two children, a boy and a girl.

The day was sultry, for it was the time of the great heat.
Cicadas, hidden among the leaves of the trees along the outskirts of the village, filled the air with their loud, rasping
music. Oxen ate leisurely their chopped straw, while their
masters squatted on the ground in the coolest spot of their
courtyards. Everyone held heaping bowls of coarse dough
strings in one hand and his chopsticks in the other. As the
bowls were emptied, each person went back to the untidy earthen
kitchen and filled his bowl again once, or even twice, for
there had been a bountiful wheat crop so that men could eat
to the full once more. How good the noodles tasted after
the scant crops of last year, when there had been only a limited amount of fall grain, such as corn, kao-liang, and soybeans. Everyone was so busy eating and smacking his lips
each time he chewed that there was little time for conversation. Half-starved, mangy dogs watched those bowls of steaming hot food with hungry, pleading eyes, hoping that a bite
might fall for them to snatch away.

Grandma Chang licked her chopsticks clean and sent the
little boy to the kitchen with her empty bowl. It was the duty
of her son's wife to wash the dishes and put the kitchen in

14

order. The old lady tottered out to the narrow alley, which was shaded from the blazing sun of noon by the mud wall of her courtyard. With many groans and grunts, she seated herself cross-legged on the ground and began to fan vigorously

Faithful Chang

with her ancient palm leaf fan. Occasionally she wiped the moisture from her face with the tail of her worn and faded jacket which had been left unbuttoned because the day was so hot.

Soon Grandpa Chang, wearing only baggy trousers and ragged cloth shoes, came shuffling along, for he could not bear to be far away from his companion. He squatted down with his back leaning against the big wooden gate and was soon dozing. As he slept, his mouth stood wide open showing a few scattered, snaggy teeth. The flies crawled in and out of his mouth and walked over his nose and sat on his eyelids. Grandma Chang talked idly of this and that, but he was so accustomed to her chatter all day long that it never disturbed him.

Presently, fat Mrs. Li came panting up the alley, waddling along on her little bound feet with her shoes run over at the heels. She called out in her loud, cheery voice, "Old mother, have you finished eating already? Did you have wheaten food today also? I do declare I would die of the heat if I stayed in my courtyard. Is there a breath of air here?"

"Truly it is hot enough to kill one!" replied Grandma Chang. "How many bowls did you empty this noon?"

Grandfather Chang stretched lazily and reached for his summer coat which he threw over his bare shoulders. He wiped his dripping head and face on the sleeve of his clean white garment. There was no soap in the Chang home, and water was getting to be scarce since the rains had been light again so that little could be used for washing clothes, and the coat was somewhat dingy looking. The ash-water which his son's wife used when she washed did make their things look cleaner than most of the neighbors wore, though, so Mr. Chang felt very respectable and satisfied that life was as pleasant as it was.

Mrs. Li sat down near the old couple, crossed her short legs, and squinted at her needle as she held it up to the light to see how to thread it. She ran the needle through her stringy, uncombed hair before each stitch to oil it so that it would go through the thick layers of stiff cloth which she was quilting for a shoe sole.

The two women talked of food, the weather, and the crops. Then they spoke of the shortcomings of their sons' wives. Before long, they were exchanging juicy bits of gossip.

Grandpa Chang drew his long bamboo pipe from the coarse girdle wrapped about his thin waist to hold his trousers in place. Carefully he filled the tiny brass bowl of the pipe with a few pinches of tobacco leaves. Then he lighted it, took a few puffs and lay the pipe down, whereupon Grandma Chang reached for the long stem and took her turn.

Neighbor Wang, hearing the voices, joined the group until the day was cool enough for him to return to his field. Others came along, too, their breath fragrant with the odor of onions and garlic, and their unwashed garments smelling of sweat from unbathed bodies.

Some half-grown boys scampered up the alley. Their brown, naked bodies were still wet from the slimy water of the old pool beneath the willows which was fast going dry. They threw themselves down in the dust beside their elders; then all talked breathlessly at the same time, for they had exciting news—Mr. Hwo was going to open a school and give instruction to boys! One of the boys, a tall, slender lad of ten, was so timid that he did not dare open his eyes more than half way when he spoke to anyone.

"Grandfather," he said hesitatingly, " I want to read books and learn to write characters with a brush."

"None of your family has ever gone to school, so why should you? Are you better than they?" Grandma Chang spoke sharply before Grandpa could reply in his cracked, quavering voice.

"Your food must come from the soil, my boy. The Changs have always been farmers."

"Little Son!" called a gentle voice from just inside the wall, "your young sister is awake. Come and take her out to play so that I need not be hindered in my work."

"Mother," the lad coaxed, "may I go to school? I do want book learning. I will be very obedient and industrious if you will get my father to promise that I may study books."

"My son," the mother replied gently, "I understand, but I fear that we are too poor. We cannot get along without the fuel you gather for cooking our food. Your grandparents are getting so old and feeble that they do not have the strength to mind the baby. We really cannot do without you. I am sorry that our home cannot afford a scholar."

The boy blinked back tears of disappointment and swallowed a few times as he led his little sister out to the road where the other children played. Some were tossing smooth pebbles with one hand and could keep two, and even three, or more of the little round stones in the air at one time, catching them one by one as they came down and throwing them up again without missing a single catch for several counts.

Some of the girls carried a baby brother or sister in the front of their garments. They balanced themselves on one tiny, crippled foot, while with the other foot, they tossed a cash which had some brightly colored chicken feathers fastened in the hole in the middle. As this feathered toy fell within kicking distance it was sent up again. It was not allowed to touch the ground, the player counting aloud all the while to see who could keep the feathers flying the longest.

The children screamed and shouted and quarreled while they played. Son, being meek and patient like his mother, would neither quarrel nor fight with the others. He quietly took Little Sister back into their own tiny court whenever an angry dispute started. Because he was so kind, the other children often deceived and took advantage of him.

Girls who would soon be of marriageable age stayed modestly within the shelter of their own homes. The boys and younger girls played in the streets at night, and they ran into any home where their fancy led them and there was no cross dog to keep them out. When they had scurried here and there until they were ready to fall asleep from weariness, they returned to their own homes.

Instead of playing with the others, old Chang's grandson went to the Hwo home. He would steal silently into the room where Teacher Hwo sat on a stiff wooden chair, bent over a black lacquered table, reading by a flickering bean oil lamp. Everyone said that Teacher Hwo had a whole stomach full of characters. An admiring group of neighbors went to his home in the evenings. They sat on little bamboo stools or squatted in the doorway while the learned old man read to them in his loud, sing-song voice. Sometimes, he paused to adjust his enormous horn spectacles or to explain the meaning of some sentence which was too deep to be understood by his ignorant listeners.

Whenever the teacher grew thirsty from reading such a long time, he felt of the tea pot. If he found the tea too cool to be fit for drinking, he poured it out on the earthen floor.

Faithful Chang as a Water Carrier

When Mrs. Hwo saw him she always hurried to the tea shop for another pot of boiling water. The Chang boy leaned against the teacher's chair and looked over his shoulder as he read. He did this, night after night, and week after week, until he could recognize many of the characters himself.

The drought became more threatening with the passing of the weeks. There was little hope of an autumn crop, and the wheat could not be planted. Mother went to the temple even when she was too busy to spare the time. She burned incense and implored the gods to have pity.

Even Grandmother, leaning heavily upon her gnarled stick, made her withered and rheumatic old legs painfully carry her to the temple. She sometimes fell headlong while trying to force her stiff knees to bend sufficiently before the idols so that she could touch the ground with her forehead again and again. Every morning a fresh stick was added to the little earthen pot of smoldering incense ash. The incense pot stood on a tiny shelf just under the fly-specked, smoke-grimed god which was pasted to the mud wall. In spite of the incense burned and the vows made, the idols were unrelenting. The longed-for rains did not fall.

The boy and his father gathered fuel every day for cooking their food, wherever they could find it—leaves, sticks, roots, weeds, and straws. At night the two of them went out to steal anything they came upon which could be eaten. Most nights they went to bed with hunger pains gnawing at their stomachs. Their bedding was insufficient for the cold of winter, so they took off their wadded garments and spread them on top of the quilts. The heat from the kettle took the chill off the brick k'ang where the grandparents slept, but there was not enough fuel to heat the other beds. The rest of the family pulled the worn quilts over their heads and shivered through the long hours of darkness.

Even though the Changs were so poor, matches had to be

21

bought and oil for the tiny lamp. Son ran such errands for his mother and usually managed to keep back a cash or two for himself without his elders suspecting it.

One morning a bookseller visited the village of Shih Li Ying and Son bought one of the little books. Blunderingly he read it, but there were so many unfamiliar characters that he could not get the sense of the book until Teacher Hwo read it for him. It was full of wise sayings, and the boy marveled as he listened. The one he liked most of all was: "Surely in vain the net is spread in the sight of any bird."

Some weeks passed and again a man came to the village to sell books. Son bought another tiny book. He was spell-bound as different ones read aloud while he listened. The story of Moses was the most beautiful thing that he had ever heard. All the stories that he knew were about terrible dragons and demons and evil spirits.

When not busy with the work of the little farm, Mr. Chang and the boy would go out with large baskets. They gathered manure along the roadside, wherever they could find it. If they had a sweet-potato crop, the father would push, the boy would pull a rope tied to the front of the squeaky wheelbarrow and, in this way, they took the sweet-potatoes to market. While the father called out in a loud voice, informing passers-by that a great bargain awaited them at his wheelbarrow, the son was free to go where he would to see the strange sights of the city. Often it took the whole day to dispose of their goods; sometimes they had to take part of their load back home with them.

One day as Son walked slowly along the street, his mouth

ajar with astonishment and his eyes staring at the wonderful sights, he happened to pass by the street chapel. At first he did not know what it was. He wondered why so many people sat listening while one person was talking to them. Although he had heard many strange tales about this foreign teaching, he had never seen their chapel before. People said that the missionaries, commonly known as foreign devils, made medicine from the hearts and eyes of little children. Some even declared that children had been cut into large pieces and pickled in earthen crocks. He decided to watch and see what kind of folk dared go inside.

Son stood at the open door and looked in.

"Don't be afraid," said the kind-faced man who was speaking. "You see we have comfortable benches here, and we invite you to come inside and rest while you listen."

The young man hastily glanced around to see if any of the neighbors might chance to be passing. When he saw that there were only strange faces in the crowd near the door, he had courage to go inside. Evangelist Wang Feng Ming told the story of Lazarus and the rich man that day. His friendly, cheerful manner completely won young Chang's confidence. Every time there was a market, the young man watched for an opportunity to hear more, but his father was always angry and scolded him when he found that he had been at the street chapel.

"Tomorrow will be Sunday, and I wish to invite you to come to the mission chapel at Twin Street, which is in the east suburb," announced Evangelist Wang one Saturday afternoon.

The next morning young Chang slipped away from the

house and went to the mission alone. As he reached the big gate, a round-faced, pleasant-looking man invited him to come into the gate house and rest until time for the service. A cup of hot tea was poured for him, and the kind man gave him an attractive booklet to take home with him. During the last few years he had learned more characters so could read ordinary books. So great was his thirst for knowledge that he had bought other books but, after reading this one, he had no more use for the "empty" ones, whereupon he burned them.

When the boy asked his father for permission to go to the mission the next Sunday, the father reviled him for wanting to idle away his time. But young Chang had such an insatiable longing to hear more that he took the big fuel basket on his arm and started out as though he were only going to work. After he had cut enough grass and weeds to nearly fill the basket, he hid it in some rushes while he attended the morning service. He did this, not just once, but many times.

One hot afternoon when Son reached home, his father cursed him and would not let him eat even a mouthful of the coarse, unleavened bread. He ordered him to go out immediately and gather more fuel. Another Sunday when he came home late, weary and hungry, his father sent him out to watch the kao-liang field for the night, fearing the neighbors would steal his crop, even as he had stolen theirs. When the father was not watching, the patient mother took her boy some cold, dark bread and some green onion tops to eat with it. She also carried a pot of hot water.

For two years young Chang had been engaged to a girl just two years younger than himself. His grandparents had died so that there was more room now. His parents thought that it was high time a boy of nineteen should be married. The family was too poor to hire sedan chairs from the city so two ox carts were made ready by sweeping them clean and spreading a clean thick quilt on the bottom of each cart. Two oxen, one in front of the other, were hitched to each of the carts.

The woman of ceremonies rode in one cart, and the groom and his attendants in another. The bridegroom wore a bright red sash crossed over his shoulders and tied around the waist of his new blue gown. Since it was still quite dark, they took four large paper lanterns to light the way to the bride's home.

The girl had bowed to her friends the night before. Then she had bowed to the ancestral shrine and gone to her room to weep. She had risen very early on her wedding morning, for her long braid of straight black hair must be carefully combed and platted in a coil at the back of her neck. There were new earrings with bright pink pendants and a pretty cloth flower for her hair. She knew by the crowing of the roosters in the village that the carts would soon be there. The bride looked very sweet in her pretty flowered cotton trousers and her bright red jacket.

The lumbering carts drew near the big gate, and the drivers' loud "whoa!" rang out on the morning air. Quickly the girl's face was covered with a bright red silk handkerchief, and the attendants carried her out in a rickety old chair, for it was not modest for her to walk to the cart. After the woman of ceremonies had burned incense in the cart to drive out any evil spirits that might be lurking there to do mischief, the bride was lifted to the cart. When she had gone, the groom paid his respects to her parents by bowing before them with his face to the ground.

The banging of firecrackers announced the arrival of the wedding party at the Chang home. The bride was again carried in a chair to the bridal chamber, pausing in the court long enough to bow with her husband before his parents, and then they bowed to heaven.

Fresh, white paper had been pasted over the lattice window, and large sheets of bright red paper on which the "hsi" character, meaning joy, or happiness, had been written, were pasted on the big outer gate, also on the door of the room. There were new straw mats on the brick bed and some pretty new quilts. They were neatly folded to show the beauty of their floral designs and stacked against the wall at the back of the k'ang.

The bride's face remained covered throughout the wedding ceremony so that her husband did not know how attractive she was until the guests left that night and he could go to the room they were to share together. Since his engagement had been made through middle-men and one can seldom believe half what they say, the young man was surprised at the beauty of his wife.

The next morning, the new daughter-in-law arose early and combed her hair with a wooden comb. Then she patted on a little more oily perfume and adjusted her hair ornaments. After she had washed her face and hands in steaming hot water and dusted a bit of powder on her face, she went before her husband's parents and bowed low and gracefully.

The groom's family had already sent a present to the bride's parents the day before. There were two kinds of meat, two kinds of fruit, noodles, and lily root—eight articles in all—two of a kind. After the morning meal of millet gruel and steamed bread, the ox cart was hitched, and the new couple went to visit her parents. All of those who had assisted at the wedding in any way were invited to attend the feast. The bride, as was fitting for one newly wed, sat modestly with downcast eyes and did not take part in the conversation.

The new wife did not object to her husband going to the mission, neither did his mother. Although his father continued to persecute him, he went whenever he could manage to do so and became a Christian about one year after his marriage. It was during a station class that his heart was so moved upon that he wept bitterly because he felt the load of his sins. He went home to make restitution to his parents. Never did he gamble, and never did he revile again, even at the New Year season when so many people gamble for pastime.

A Christian evangelist who had been a devout Buddhist before his conversion gave the young Christian a new name, "Teh Tao," which means, "obtained the doctrine." Even the neighbors saw the change in the young man although he had never been so very evil.

"Young Chang has surely eaten the foreign devil's medicine now," remarked the village folk to each other. "Just see how he wastes time going to the mission."

Teh Tao added a little son to the family so there were now five mouths to feed, including his parents. Crops had not been good since the year he brought his bride home. The proud father had just read the story of Joseph for the first time, and where could one find a nicer name for a son?

Since no work could be found near home, and it was rumored that men were being hired to mine coal in Manchuria, Joseph's father walked many miles to reach the railroad, hoping to travel the rest of the way on one of the fast fire wagons. He waited for several days, his few pieces of silver melting away all too fast, although he bought only the cheapest kind of food and not enough to satisfy his hunger. At last word came that there would be no more travel to Manchuria until the plague, which was killing people by the hundreds, was stayed. There was nothing for Teh Tao to do but return to his home.

Ten days later a friend found employment for the young man at the mission station. His work was to sweep the chapel and the courtyard and to carry water in two big buckets fastened, one at each end, to a long carrying pole. There was much water to carry since the large water jars must be kept filled in the homes of the teachers and evangelists. Then a number of Christians were staying at the mission while they received instruction in the doctrine. So faithfully did he work that one year later he was given the privilege of attending classes for half of each day while his pay was not reduced.

When Joseph's little sister, Yo Ch'in, was born, the missionary-nurse went to the Chang home. Her loving care created a desire in the heart of young Mrs. Chang to go to the mission herself. As soon as the baby was old enough to be taken out, the young mother and her mother-in-law took the two babies and went to meeting.

Teh Tao's mother drank in the new teaching like a sponge. Her heart opened up like a flower in the sunshine. Later she was sent to minister to the women inquirers at one of the big tents.

Chang Teh Tao has served as gate-evangelist in several of our outstations. There was never a more willing or faithful worker than he. Ten years ago he was sent to Sangachen. There was no janitor there, so he swept the chapel and the courtyards; he ran errands and visited the sick; he taught new converts to pray and to sing; he dealt with inquirers and filled the pulpit; he preached in the villages. Whatever he did, he went at it with the same grace and zeal, so that we came to speak of him as "Faithful Chang."

One Saturday there was a heavy snow storm. We wondered how any one could go to Chengchia, six miles away, to lead their Sunday meeting. It was not Mr. Chang's turn to go, but he quickly offered, "Let me go. I am strong and can walk through the snow. I will go this afternoon and spend the night there."

Usually Chinese are reluctant to venture out when there is danger of getting their cloth shoes wet, but Mr. Chang was too unselfish to think of the damage that would be done to his shoes. When he did not come home Sunday night we felt a little worried about him, for there were many robbers in that section. By the middle of the next morning when he still had not appeared, the evangelist suggested that it was time for someone to start a search, lest something had befallen him. After a moment he questioned, "Could it be that the Lord has come?" There was no doubt in his mind about Chang Teh Tao being caught away at the Rapture.

Joseph has grown into a fine, dependable lad and has served as student-evangelist for two years. He attended the Short Term Bible School for three and one-half years and planned to go to the Tientsin Bible Seminary next year. To keep from being a soldier under the Conquerors, he has entered a government school conducted by army officers who move from place to place as danger arises. He is doing volunteer work on Sunday. He is engaged to a splendid Christian girl, and both of them have hearts set to follow the Lord.

Faithful Chang labored on at Sangachen, even after support was cut off from America. He put his very best into the work for ten long years, and the people of Sangachen were loathe to see him go. They could not support a gate evangelist in addition to their preacher and his wife, so Mr. Chang returned to his home where he works as a volunteer as he has opportunity. When the people saw that Mr. Chang must leave, the old women wept over him. The men made a farewell feast consisting of cabbage and meat cooked together and eaten with white steamed rolls.

Mother Chang could not stand the hardships of working at the tent as she grew older, but she faithfully works for the Lord in her own village. The farm is still small and the soil is alkaline, so Mr. Chang will have to work very hard to eke out a living from the ground.

The whole Chang family, even Father Chang, are now followers of the Jesus doctrine, and a meeting is held in the Chang home each evening. Twenty-seven years ago, there was not a single Christian in the village. Now there are more than ten homes in which one can find followers of Christ.

Joseph was attending the Tientsin Bible Seminary in 1943, when we last heard of him.

THE MAN WHO READS WITH HIS FINGERS

PEOPLE WERE pushing this way and that, and the blind fortune-teller found it rather difficult to keep himself balanced on his tiny camp stool. Above the din of voices, the squeaking of wheelbarrows, the braying of donkeys, and the cry of vendors calling their wares, a sweet melody reached his ear. Surely it could not be the theatrical performers, for in all his twenty-five years he had never heard anything as beautiful. It sounded like some one singing something about love, but surely his ears were deceiving him. There was no such thing as love. He stood to his feet and turned his head that he might catch the sound more clearly. What did they say? "Jesus Loves Me"? It certainly sounded like that, but what could it mean? "Who is Jesus, anyway?" pondered the blind man.

He quickly folded his camp stool and tucked it under one arm. Throwing his bedding roll and the paraphernalia he used when he told fortunes over the other shoulder, he hurried off in the direction from which the music was coming. He pressed his way through the throng until he came in contact with a tent pole, which he leaned against to keep himself from being thrust aside by the crowd.

Hour after hour went by, and he was losing money, but still he listened. The evangelist told about a God of love, and one radiant Christian after another testified to having found peace and happiness in serving this God whose name was Jesus. But could it be possible that he, a poor blind man with only a hard life before him, could find happiness? Life had looked bright enough until that unlucky day five years before when the gods had smitten him with blindness for some sin.

"You have been standing here so long that you must be very tired," a kind voice said. "Some of the people have started for home now, and I think that I can find you a seat on the other side. Let me lead you over there, and I will bring you a bowl of hot water, for you must be thirsty."

The old grey-haired Bible woman, Mrs. Tu, reached out her hand to grasp the crooked stick which the man used for a cane. She found a place for him to sit on one of the narrow, backless benches. Then she went to the little table at the front of the room where there was a tea-pot. She poured the cool water from a bowl on the ground, and feeling of the tea-pot found that it was still hot enough, so she carried a coarse bowl in both her hands and gave it to the young man, who drank thirstily.

All four days of the fair the fortune-teller stayed by the tent. He even spread out his quilt and slept there on the cold ground at night. He heard them say that one could have eternal life if he would forsake his sins and believe in Jesus.

Mr. Liu prayed for forgiveness. Then he felt his way with his walking stick to the little mud hut one mile away, where he had lived alone since his father's death the winter before. His mother had died when he was a wee lad of five. There were no brothers in the home, for all of them had died while infants. He groped around the untidy room until the last paper god was torn from the smoke-blackened walls and burned.

Mr. Liu was so happy to know that there was one who loved him that he wanted to tell some one else of the wonderful experience which had come to him. He went to the home of a relative with whom he had quarreled.

"Aunt," he said, "I will take all of the blame for our misunderstanding. It was all my fault. I have become a Christian, and I wish that you, too, would believe in Jesus. He is the true God, and He can give you rest and peace in your heart."

"You have lost your mind, sure enough!" the aunt screamed angrily. "Here you have wasted four whole days listening to those crazy people who are following the foreign devils when you might have taken in several strings of cash to help tide you over the winter. It is not every day that such an opportunity comes to make money. There will not be another theater here in a good many moons. You need not come to me for food this winter after having idled away your time in this fashion. My house is full of children anyway, and we have more mouths than we can feed."

And in her anger she spat on the dirt floor and made an ugly face. The children were quarreling and making an uproar. She reached out her rough hand and slapped the one nearest her and sent it bawling from the room. She felt in her deep bosom and found a copper which she gave to the baby to buy some peanuts. She scolded first one and then another of the children, and Mr. Liu left without waiting to drink even a bowl of hot water.

The blind man heard that a station class was to begin the next day at a town four miles from his home. During the week a market town about a mile from this village was to have a four days' fair. He was so eager to hear more of the "Jesus doctrine" that he decided to go to the class and listen until his money was gone—he had almost one dollar left—then he would go to the fair and tell fortunes to earn more.

I went to the chapel one frosty morning before time for the first class of the day in order to become acquainted with some who had come early. People warmed their hands over a charcoal fire in a little earthen pot, for the room was cold. The Bible woman, Mrs. Tu, was explaining a simple song

The fortune-teller always carried his belongings in a small bag. The Bible woman had kindly offered to put it in her room where it would be safe. She had scarcely finished explaining the song when Mr. Liu asked her to bring the bag to him. While she was gone to fetch it a lad who sat near the blind man led him by the hand to the front of the room where the coals were burning, for the man had asked some one to lead him to the fire.

As Mrs. Tu put the bag into the man's hand, he opened it and removed one article after another, putting them into the fire. The people were amazed and wondered what was wrong with the man. One even grabbed his arm to stop him, while others quickly gathered about him.

"How will you live?" asked one. "You spent money and studied in school to learn how to tell fortunes."

"Don't burn all those things," cried another. "Stop him!

That thing could be used for a pencil holder. Why, it's worth a whole silver piece! Don't let him burn it!"

"I am through with it. It belongs to the devil. I wash my hands of all this," replied Mr. Liu.

"But what will you do? How will you eat?" some one asked.

"I will go out and beg before I will continue to deceive people. I can't go on with this work, and believe in the Lord at the same time."

A Christian gave the blind man another dollar, so he followed us to the next station class which was only a few miles farther on, and he said that he would become a beggar when the money was all gone.

We learned that Mr. Liu had been a foreman in a cloth factory in Tientsin, where he had been getting a very good salary. He became exceedingly angry when a friend who owed him twenty dollars left the city without returning the money. From that time on his eye-sight began to fail quite rapidly. He went to a Chinese doctor who punctured one eyeball with a needle, and there seemed to be no hope for the other eye.

I could not bear to think of this bright young man becoming a beggar without first having had an opportunity to do something else, so invited him to come to my station for a few weeks and study the Braille system of reading. Within a few days he had learned to read and write, and in two or three months he had read the four gospels and the first fifteen chapters of Acts. The blind evangelist, Mr. An, explained to him the meaning of the book of John, verse by verse, and he memorized the whole of it. He also learned to sing many beautiful hymns.

So concerned was Mr. Liu that others might hear the Good News that he started out from village to village, visiting first his relatives and friends. People marveled that one who was blind could read. They came running from all parts of the village to watch him read with his fingers. Then they gladly stayed to listen to his message and his songs, for he sang with a good clear voice which people liked to hear.

When we were interned at the beginning of the war between America and Japan, we were left in the mission compound with Chinese guards, as the Japanese were afraid to be outside the city walls after night. However, they came freely during the day.

When Mr. Liu learned that we were imprisoned, he hurried to the place. It was late in the afternoon and the Japanese soldiers had all returned to the city. The Chinese guards did not hinder him when he came to see us. At first he spoke some words of comfort, and then he told us that he wanted to help us in our time of need. He had given his time to evangelistic work, going from one mission station to another, sometimes walking for two or three days at a time and conducting a service wherever he stopped. Usually some one offered him food after hearing his testimony, although many times it was the first time that they had ever heard the Christian religion. Sometimes the Christians have given him money for his travel, even paying for a railroad ticket.

Mr. Liu was well dressed that afternoon, most of his clothing being new. His face glowed as he told us of God's goodness to him and pointed to each of his garments, telling how his hat and his coat, his new trousers, and even his socks and his shoes had been given to him by some child of God. He reached into his pocket and pulled out two one dollar bills. Holding them out to us he said, "You will not be able to get money from America now, so I want to help you. The Christians of one congregation have given me twenty dollars for railroad and bus fare. They have asked me to come to them for a meeting. I can walk to the railroad station in three days or so and give you the money that it would take for my bus fare. I have another two dollars for the Richards."

As we looked into that happy face and listened to Mr. Liu's joyous testimony, we rejoiced that a poor, helpless blind man had found peace in this life with the hope of eternal bliss awaiting him. His needs have been better supplied than they would ever have been had he continued to serve Satan and tell fortunes. When we refused to accept his money, he gave it to the Chinese workers, for he felt that he wanted to help in some way.

For more than ten years, Mr. Liu has been going about from place to place supported entirely by those of the Chinese who are interested in him and appreciate his ministry. Most of his relatives have now become Christians, even the aunt. Although Mr. Liu can never hope to see again with his natural eyes, his face glows with joy as he says, "I once was blind, but now I see."

IN A DARK little mud house a man lay dying. His body was wasted by illness, and he lay on his brick bed with his mouth wide open, gasping for every breath. Slowly, ever so slowly, his dimming eyes searched the room until his gaze rested upon his white-haired mother. The seventy bitter winters through which she had passed had deeply lined her sad face.

A five-year-old little daughter stood anxiously watching her mother who went to the bedside and bent over the sick man, giving him some bitter herb tea with the hope that it would help him. The child's mother wiped the unbidden tears from her eyes. Life had never been kind to her. She grew up in a home of poverty and became the bride of a man whose family was as poor as her own. Her husband had worked hard, and she had gone to the field during busy times to help him with the planting and the hoeing. Toil as they would, there were times when they could not make ends meet, for the little farm was small, and the soil was not productive. How could she ever get along if she must do the work by herself?

The Aheng (priest) came from the mosque and began to read the Koran. Like most of the homes in the village of Hsu Chieh Yao, this was a Mohammedan one. There was no idol of any kind and no incense was ever burned. There was never any kowtowing, to either the living or the dead. At the New Year time red coloring had been faithfully smeared at the sides and on the lintel of the door. No one ate meat dumplings before the second day of the holiday season lest he inadvertently eat pork. Most Chinese used pork for their New Year feast, but a good Mohammedan would die rather than touch it. Mr. Small-gate had observed the customs of the mosque from childhood.

In her grief, the old mother rocked back and forth while an occasional sob escaped her lips. As the sick man breathed his last, she began to wail, "My son! Oh, my son! How can we get along without you?"

One spring afternoon six months after her father's death, the little daughter came in with her hands full of pussy willows. Seeing smoke pouring from the kitchen, she supposed that her mother must be there. As she looked in at the open door, there sat her grandmother before the kettle.

"Where is my mother?" asked the child.

"She is resting in the next room. Go quickly and see the nice present she has for you!"

"Mother, mother!" cried the child. "Have you something for me?"

"Here, daughter, come up close and you shall see."

The child had never seen her mother resting in the daytime before, but there she lay on the very same brick bed where the father had died. As she saw the tired look on her mother's thin, pale face, fear gripped her little heart for a moment. Was her mother going to die? The thought had no more than formed itself when she heard a baby's cry!

Grandmother came in all smiles and helped the child climb up on the k'ang beside her new brother.

Although the young widow had slaved from early to late to feed and clothe the three of them, there had never been quite enough. How would she feed four mouths? But with

Evangelist Small-gate with His Motherless Children

a son to care for her in her declining years, she could face the future more hopefully.

Times grew worse for the little family the next few years. The grandmother went to spend a winter at the home of a maternal relative where there was more to eat. Since she became very feeble there, she stayed on until her death. When the little girl was ten the mother engaged her to a Mohammedan's son.

Mrs. Small-gate looked upon her son as such a priceless treasure that she never made any attempt to govern him. Being too poor to go to school, the boy did not have the discipline of a schoolmaster. He followed his own inclinations. Things reached such a state one day, however, that the mother saw she must take her self-willed boy in hand. Looking about the room for something to lay her hand on, she seized the handleless kaffir-corn broom. The boy dived for the brick bed. Drawing the ragged quilt over his head, he crouched there trembling and sobbing in anger. When his mother pulled the cover off, he ran screaming into the yard. Just beyond the little courtyard was a road, and beside this road was a large open well where all the neighbors came for their water. The obstinate lad ran toward the well. "I'm going to drown myself!" he shrieked at the top of his voice. "You can't beat me with that broom!"

"You pig, you," screamed the mother in loud, angry tones. Being a good Mohammedan, this was her way of reviling. She could think of nothing worse than a pig.

There were a few people at the well, but the boy considered them neither sufficient in number nor interest to put forth much effort to rescue a drowning person. He fully intended to jump into that well, but he had no intention of drowning. While playing for time, he wound his pigtail around his head so that it would not catch on the rough bricks of the well. Then he rolled his trouser legs a little tighter, yelling all the while to attract more people.

Hearing the screams, people hurried toward the well. Venders set their baskets down. Women with hair awry hurried out of their yards, wiping their hands on their aprons as they rushed to the spot, while flocks of dirty, ragged children came running at their heels. There being no excuse for further delay, the boy elbowed his way through the crowd until he was at the edge of the well.

The mother saw that her precious one really meant to leap into the well. She clung to him and tried to drag him away, but her strength was no match for the eight-year-old boy whose heart was filled with rage. The neighbors restrained the lad and coaxed him to go into the house with his mother. Mrs. Small-gate was worn out with the struggle and panted for breath as she declared to those assembled, "I'll never try to control him again."

When Ch'ing En was fourteen years old, he stole a pumpkin from a neighbor's garden. When accused, he did not admit his guilt but secretly watched for an opportunity to take revenge. One day during the heat of noon when most folk were napping in the shade, the boy looked around and saw that no one was watching. He dashed into the pumpkin patch and broke about forty pumpkins, large and small, from the vines. At first, the owner did not notice what had happened, but when he did, he went to the road outside Widow Small-gate's home and cursed the boy and all of his relatives.

Of course, Ch'ing En denied any knowledge of the deed, but his mother did not feel satisfied that he was innocent.

She was afraid to say anything, but she prepared no food for her son or herself that evening, and he knew that this was his punishment. The sister had married a few years before so there was no one else at home.

About a week later, Ch'ing En hid a big kitchen knife in his clothing. After he had looked this way and that, he split open a few of the pumpkins, leaving them fastened together as though nothing had happened. The neighbor did not know that anything was wrong until he was ready to sell his pumpkins at the market, and he found them mouldy and rotten inside.

When the Small-gate boy was nearly nineteen, he stole a big watermelon from Neighbor Ts'ai's. Upon being questioned as to where it came from, he told his mother that he had bought it for a few coppers. When Mr. Ts'ai discovered that his finest melon was gone, he felt sure that he knew who had taken it. Going to the gate of the Small-gate home, he stood there, bawling out thieves in a high shrill voice that all the neighbors could hear. Ch'ing En stayed in the house, but his anger was mounting.

The next summer, Mr. Ts'ai's wheat was piled high on the threshing-floor in front of his house, waiting for the ox to tramp over it dragging the heavy stone roller that would help thresh it out. Ch'ing En listened carefully, until he was sure by the deep regular breathing of his mother that she was fast asleep. He went to the threshing-floor and set fire to the wheat, then slunk away to his little mud house and crawled into bed again. Soon the blaze was high. The neighbors threw their clothes about them as they ran for the fire. Every one worked hard to save the man's wheat, Ch'ing En the hardest of any of them to prove his innocence, but he secretly rejoiced that more than ten bushels of the wheat had been destroyed.

When autumn came, Neighbor Ts'ai stacked his kao-liang leaves in one corner of his yard to cure them for feeding his ox during the winter. The leaves had been tied in bundles and were getting quite dry. Ch'ing En knew the dog so well that it did not make one "yap" when he climbed into the yard while the family were sound asleep. The roar of the fire awakened the whole house, but it was too late to save the leaves. Ts'ai suspected the bad boy but did not dare accuse him.

Ch'ing En hired an ox to plow his little wheat field and was ready to sow the seed. His cousin had a large flock of chickens, six in all, and they just would scratch in that newly plowed ground. He feared that they would ruin his entire crop, and he could not afford to have that happen. There was no money to buy fertilizer, but all that could be collected during the summer had been carefully saved and dried. He cut it into tiny bits and mixed the wheat seed with it. He spent a few cents for powdered arsenic which he stirred into the seed. Then he walked through the length and breadth of his tiny field carrying the heavy seed basket with one hand while he scattered his seed with the other, patiently watching the chickens as they scratched in the soft earth.

That very day before the sun went down, three of the cousin's hens had suddenly died. The cousin called out in anger, "Who poisoned my chickens?"

"I did," answered Ch'ing En, "because you did not care when you knew that they were scratching out my wheat."

The cousin had some grown sons who were ready to help their father give Ch'ing En a sound thrashing which they felt he richly deserved. He fled to his own home, and they did not follow him.

From that time, Ch'ing En carried a big knife concealed in his clothing. Ten days passed before the mother discovered the knife, and when she did her heart was full of fear. She asked her son why he had the knife. "It is to kill my cousin," he declared. "The big rabbit!"

"My son," the mother pleaded, as she knelt on the earth floor beside the wobbly bench where the boy sat, while the tears rained down her cheeks, "Have you no fear of the law? Don't you know that you will have your head severed from your body if you kill your cousin? Oh, my boy, have pity on your mother."

When the mother saw that her son showed no concern for her tears, she hurried to a second cousin's and begged him to come to her help. The man went with her and exhorted the wayward boy.

"Ch'ing En," he reasoned, "think how your poor mother has suffered during these bitter years since your father died, having to feed and clothe you until you were large enough to help her. You know that the lot of a widow is a hard one."

"Son," sobbed the mother, "if you do not give that knife to your second-cousin, I will cut my throat right here before you both."

Ch'ing En knew that folk would hate him and call him an

unfilial son if he grieved his mother so deeply that she took her life. Slowly, with a hard rebellious look, he handed the knife to the relative saying, "We'll fight it out another day. I shall have my revenge."

Second-cousin was a soldier who had secured a three-day leave of absence, and he had to return to the army. He did not come home again for three or four years. When he came that time, he stayed the whole winter. He told them that while he was far from home he had gone to a mission and heard the Jesus doctrine. Some one told him that there was a Jesus chapel in the city of Tungchangfu, just six li away. When he was asked about the teaching of this new doctrine he replied, "Why, all countries have the Jesus church now. I only heard two or three times while I was away but I'd like to go again. Come along, Ch'ing En, and hear them once for yourself."

Ch'ing En did not want to go to the street chapel with his cousin so tried to find excuses for not going. He had often passed by on market days and sneeringly remarked, "The foreign dogs are barking again today." But his cousin persuaded him to go with him once. He was not particularly attracted but felt that he would like to go again and went in alone on another market day.

Evangelist Wang Feng Ming was the preacher that day. He told his listeners that those who reviled or struck their parents would go to hell. He said that burning incense and abstaining from certain kinds of food, even pork, could save no one. Sinners must repent and be respectful to their parents. Ch'ing En bowed his head in shame and considered. He had been taught that there was a heaven and a hell. "Could such a wicked one as he go to heaven?" he wondered. After the others had gone, he sat deep in thought for a few moments, then slowly arose and started to leave.

"What is your honorable name and where do you live?" asked Evangelist Wang.

"My unworthy name is Tou Ch'ing En, and my humble home is in the village of Hsu Chieh Yao."

Evangelist Wang saw that the young man was troubled so walked a short distance with him. He knew that there were many Mohammedans in that part of the country who were members of the Small-gate clan, so he asked, "You are a Mohammedan, aren't you?"

"Would it do for a Mohammedan to believe in Jesus?" questioned Ch'ing En.

"It would be easier for you than for others. You have no false gods, therefore your sins are fewer. Come to the mission next Sunday and hear more."

It took courage, but Ch'ing En went to the Sunday meeting and took two others with him, his second cousin and a friend, Wu P'ei Sheng. After they had attended meetings for a few Sundays, Evangelist Wang said to them, "You have heard enough to understand something of this doctrine. Would you like to become Christians now?"

Being timid about praying, they knelt and asked the Lord to forgive them for reviling and a few such common sins, but no peace came to their hearts.

A few weeks later, the first big tent came from America. It was pitched at Tungchangfu. Ch'ing En listened very earn-

47

estly for a day or two, and then he and his two companions repented to the very bottom. They could not come to the night meetings but met together in Ch'ing En's home where they sang the few songs that they had been learning, read the Bible by a flickering bean-oil lamp and prayed. Since they did not know what to pray about, they confessed their sins to God every night.

Widow Small-gate was pleased over the change in her bad boy. He had now become an obedient son. She began going to the Jesus Chapel herself but was afraid to openly become a Christian. She feared that she might unwittingly eat some food which had been cooked in a kettle defiled by pork if she mingled too freely with the Christians. She believed that the eating of pork would close heaven's gate to her forever.

Ch'ing En became a janitor at the mission and was later promoted to a missionary's kitchen. His testimony had a true ring, and he knew that he was really born again. One morning when the missionary went to the kitchen and told him about a very good meeting she had been in, the tears filled his eyes. The most convenient thing to wipe his eyes on happened to be the tea-towel. He used it.

About that time Ch'ing En heard the evangelist say that if we offended our brother we should ask his pardon. He thought of the poisoned chickens the first thing and asked to be excused from his work so that he could visit the cousin. After prayer he started on his errand. As he reached the gate, his courage almost failed him. He implored God to help him and then went inside the gate. As soon as he had entered the yard, he saw the cousin sitting in the doorway. There was no turning back!

"Cousin," he hurried to say, "I was such a wicked boy, but now I am a Christian. I once intended to kill you, but God has changed my heart and wants me to confess this to you. Do not be angry but please forgive me. I hope that you will go to the Jesus chapel."

The cousin was too surprised to answer immediately. When he could speak, he said, "We will not talk of the past. Let us forget it."

As the young man came out of the yard he felt as if a heavy brick had rolled from his heart. He was free and happy, and he thanked God for giving him strength. He tried to show that he was a changed man by being especially kind to those whom he had wronged.

Mr. Ch'en, the head evangelist, asked Ch'ing En to buy some soybean oil for him. There was some change left, and Ch'ing En felt that he deserved some reward for his trouble. He bought two or three little dumplings for himself, then handed the rest of the money to Mr. Ch'en when he took the oil to him. As he prayed that night, there was no peace in his heart. The next morning he went to Mr. Ch'en and confessed his wrong.

A janitor was needed at Nankwantao, and Ch'ing En was sent there to fill the vacancy. One year later he entered the training school at Tungchangfu. About that time he became engaged to a lovely little school girl whose mother was a widow. Having no way to live the widow was being married again, but she could not provide for the girl. Ch'ing En did evangelistic work the next two years, then married, his wife being about seventeen at that time. Together they took up the work at an outstation.

Soon after, Widow Small-gate died. Since a Mohammedan funeral is not contrary to Christian custom, Ch'ing En did not try to hinder the relatives in carrying out their plans. It would have been useless anyway. Although the mother had attended the Jesus chapel, she had faithfully observed the Mohammedan customs as before. Women were not permitted to worship at the mosque on Friday, the Mohammedan day of worship. There were small stalls about three feet square in the mosque. Each stall was fitted with a wooden pail, having a plug in the bottom of the pail to provide running water for ceremonial washing before worship. Washing the hands, feet, and head from a pitcher of water served for minor ablutions unless defilement had taken place. The mouth must always be washed before speaking the prayer talk.

Widow Small-gate had brought holy water from the mosque for ceremonial bathing and observed the time of prayer in her home whenever she could. Five times each day the call to prayer rang out from the mosque. 1. Adam's time came before daylight. 2. Abraham's time, just before the sun passed the meridian. 3. Jonah's time about three p.m. 4. Jesus' time about sunset. 5. Moses or Mohammed's time about nine p.m.

When it was evident that Mrs. Small-gate would not recover, the Aheng, accompanied by his wife, came to the home and read from the Koran. As the dying woman was too weak to raise the index finger of her right hand, her daughter held it up for her. This sign, "i-ma," in Chinese was her testimony that she had not worshipped idols. The sin of idolatry cannot be forgiven even on the death bed. After the death of the mother, the daughter performed the "ch'i-mi" ceremony by putting two grains of rice into each ear of the corpse, two grains under each eye-lid, two grains into the mouth, and two grains into each nostril. It is feared that any negligence connected with these rites may result in the children of the deceased giving birth to defective children.

The Aheng's wife bathed the body and then swathed it in long white bandages, adding a few fragrant spices as she wrapped each member separately. Even a child's body is wrapped rather than dressed before burial. Unless the weather is excessively hot, a Mohammedan funeral is often delayed until the third day, but even the rich do not postpone burial beyond the third day. During the three days before the funeral, there was some chanting in the home and four days more of chanting at the grave, making seven days in all. In rich homes, the chanting often lasts for forty days and sometimes as many as sixteen Ahengs take part. No wine is served at Mohammedan funerals, for the priests do not drink wine. The Aheng is given an offering for his services. It may be as little as one dollar or as much as one hundred, or even several hundred dollars, depending upon the wealth and liberality of the family. While he does not demand money, he has ways of showing his displeasure when he feels that his gift has been too small.

The body was placed on a board under which the ropes for lowering it into the grave were fixed. Then the bottomless coffin was brought from the mosque and used en route to the grave. Since the corpse was a woman, only the family could look on while the coffin was being removed. The square grave was lined with bricks, and after the son had arranged the body, the top of the grave was boarded over. Of course, the head was toward the north with the face looking toward Mecca. The children both took a handful of earth from each of the four corners of the grave and carried it home with them.

The daughter had taken a bag of thick cakes to the grave, and after the funeral she gave a piece to each person who had assisted in any capacity, whether as grave digger or pall-bearer. The carriers range in number from sixteen to thirty-two, depending upon the size of the funeral. Sometimes, there are as many as forty-eight, and they expect to be feasted for their services.

Ch'ing En and his wife had four lovely children who were taught to pray from the time that they could lisp a few words. When the oldest child, Beautiful Lilac, was eight she said to the missionary one night, "I told the other children that I was not afraid in the dark, but I am. Please help me pray that Jesus will forgive me for telling that lie."

Mrs. Small-gate was not strong, and when Fragrant Jade, the fifth child, was born they hired a wet-nurse for him. This woman nursed him at her own breast, keeping him in her home. She carried him in her bosom when he was too restless to lie on the brick bed.

Mrs. Small-gate had been sick for about one year and, for one whole month, she had not left the hard brick bed. Christmas dawned such a bright beautiful day, and the people flocked to the mission station at Hotien. The chapel had not yet been built. The large outer room of the evangelist's two-roomed home was used for the chapel, while his family were huddled in a smaller room for the winter.

Mrs. Small-gate asked for her clothes. She wanted to get up and be with those women who had come to celebrate the birth of her Lord and theirs. Her husband warmed her padded garments over a bonfire which he made by lighting a handful of dry leaves. He helped the sick woman who was too weak to dress by herself, then she staggered into the big room and greeted the women. They were so happy to see her and politely inquired about her health. Between fits of coughing, she said to them, "Don't worry about me. My illness will soon be over and, ere long, I shall be with Jesus."

Her strength was soon spent, and she was forced to go back to bed. A few days later Mrs. Small-gate said to her husband, "I have two worries—my mother and these babies." The mother had no son and this was her only child. Children are supposed to care for their parents in old age, and there would be no one to do that now. If her mother should again be left a widow, sad indeed would be her lot. She might even be driven from the home since she would have no further claim upon it.

Little Virtuous Gem, nearly six, and Bright Gem, not yet four, played happily together. The sisters, Beautiful Lilac, not quite thirteen, and Glorious Lilac, past ten, were in school at Tungchangfu nearly thirty miles away. The mother watched over her small boys with anxious eyes as they were busy at their play.

"Take good care of my children," she said to the husband. When Mr. Small-gate hurried to her side during a hard coughing spell, she said cheerfully, "It does not matter," and was gone.

The next day was Sunday. Since the sun shone brightly, the Christians came to meeting as usual. The narrow little benches were moved out into the yard. The people sat in the warmth of the sunshine, but they hardly expected a meeting. Mr. Small-gate suggested that he preach to them as he always had. He stood in the yard and led the meeting, while the mother of his children lay still and cold in death in the big, cheerless room.

The messenger returned with the girls that night. A Christian brought the huge rough coffin and helped put the corpse into it. At dawn the next morning, the clumsy unpainted box was loaded into an ox cart. Beautiful Lilac and her father accompanied the body back to the little old mud house and the tiny field where the grandparents were buried.

Beautiful Lilac has carried a heavy load these four years. She has been a mother to the other children, besides making shoes and clothing by hand, grinding grain and cooking for the family. She has been able to finish grade school and take a few classes in the Short Term Bible School, as her father has been stationed at Tungchangfu, going out on his bicycle for the village work. She is a beautiful, gifted girl, well poised and deeply spiritual. All of the children have done well under the skillful discipline of their father.

Mr. Small-gate has had to take his family back to the little farm since America entered the war. He was not well when we left. It will be difficult for him to eke out a living, but his faith is strong in God. He was one of the number who gathered at the mission compound early that June morning when we had to leave. His chin quivered, and his eyes filled with tears as he clasped his two hands together and bowed deeply, saying "Tsai chien," which means, "We will meet again."

Friends reaching America on the second trip of the Gripsholm bring word of the triumphant death of Mr. Small-gate. His five children have joined that ever growing multitude of suffering humanity—China's unfortunate war orphans.

EVERY YEAR when the twenty-third day of the twelfth moon came, the Tu family offered incense before the dirty, smoke-grimed kitchen god and burned a handful of wheat straw for his horse. They sometimes smeared something sweet on his lips, for they were getting ready to send him to heaven where he would give a report of their conduct during the past year. If they had a bowl of wine, they dipped the paper god into it, and there were times when they daubed a bit of opium on his mouth so that he would be too drowsy to remember their unkind deeds. Then they burned the god and lived without him for the next week.

During the last days of the old year, the women were busy cleaning house, preparing steamed bread and meat dumplings, and getting the clothing in order for the family so that every one might appear at his best those first days of the New Year. The men visited the itinerant barber who set up his shop on the open street. Here the customers sat on a stool while their heads were being shaved as clean as peeled onions, the hair dropping to the ground where it would. The barber sometimes paused a moment to add a lump of charcoal to the tiny stove which kept his water hot. For an extra bit of cash, he would cleanse the nostrils and ears of stray hairs and shave the eyebrows too. Occasionally one was loathe to part with his queue and insisted that his braid be freshly combed and a switch added to make it longer, but he wanted the area beyond the queue freshly shaved.

Soon after midnight on New Year's day, the new kitchen

Mr. and Mrs. Tu Huai Sheng in Winter Dress

god was pasted to the mud wall over the shelf where the old one had been. The family bowed on their faces as they welcomed the spirit of the god to their home again, and they burned incense and lighted firecrackers to make the reception more cordial. The booming of firecrackers the whole night through kept things in an unceasing uproar, and most folk did not try to sleep. Many of the men took their paper lanterns and went to the temples to pay their respects to the gods there before they started on the round of making calls.

The Tu family were devout idol worshippers, particularly, the grandparents. They used every precaution so that the evil spirits always lurking about would not harm them.

The grandmother went on long pilgrimages with the other women, and they visited all the famous temples within walking distance. Dust-covered and hair awry, these weary and hungry women often sat the whole night through on the dirty ground of some temple yard. Sometimes they watched the grey-robed priests as they came and went through the long night, bowing their shaven heads with the nine sacred scars which they received at their ordination. Great Buddhas and their attendant gods sat unmoved as clouds of incense filled the rooms and groups of monks kowtowed or chanted as they filed in and out with their measured, stately tread.

On other occasions, the women went to a Taoist temple where their fascinated gaze was fixed upon the chanting priests, dressed in rich yellow and red satin robes with their long, greasy hair knotted on top of their heads like women.

Little Huai Sheng often accompanied his grandparents to the temples. He enjoyed prostrating himself before the idols. When he was a little older, seven or eight boys, under ten years of age, helped him make a god of clay and they kowtowed to it. They stayed on their knees before it until their smoldering incense sticks had burned to the end.

When the parents of the boys gave them a copper for peanuts or sweets, they saved the money to buy incense or paper money for their god. They went to the shops of Mulberry Market Town (Sangachen), carrying a wooden tray with them, and begged coppers of the merchants for their image so that they could burn more incense to it.

About this time one of the gospel tents went to the town. The people came in great crowds at night to see the gasoline lamps, for they had never seen such bright lights. Lantern slides on the life of Christ were also a great attraction, especially for the children. The boys learned from those pictures that Jesus was the true God, and that we should not worship gods of paper, wood, or clay.

Soon after that, some missionaries moved to Mulberry Market Town, and one of them started a kindergarten for the children. They learned songs and heard about repentance. The missionary had a picture which made a deep impression on the boys who had been so zealous in idol worship. The picture showed the Christ holding a light in His hand, and underneath were some big characters which explained that Jesus is the light of the world and that only those who follow Him can be saved. Most of the boys repented as soon as they understood, and they restored to their neighbors things which they had stolen.

A teacher was invited to open a school for boys since so many of the children were eager to receive Christian instruction. Most of the parents being unable to read themselves and not realizing the benefits of an education, refused to give their boys money for slates, books, pencils and paper, until the little fellows had wept before them many times. It was customary to give the children a few coppers to spend at the fairs. The boys kept their money to buy school supplies, for they knew how hard it would be to coax more from their parents.

After the grandparents died and were buried, Mrs. Tu had a long illness and was in great pain. None of the doctor's herbs gave her relief, though she tried them all. When he gave her some white powder she was eased of her agony and could rest. She was barely thirty at the time, but the drug habit was soon formed. Day after day the woman lay upon her bed in a dark, cheerless room with the opium lamp lighted beside her, and the air was thick and heavy with the sweetish smell which filled every room of the house. She quickly smoked the flesh from her bones, growing more yellow and shrivelled every day. The little money they had melted away like so much wax.

The father still owned a bit of land, and the humble home where they lived, and these he would not sell to buy opium for his wife. His land would not produce enough to feed the three mouths, so he opened a hot water shop in the home where his neighbors came with their tea pots. For one copper coin he filled the pots with boiling water.

Mr. Tu had been fond of a cup of hot rice wine occasionally. He became so discouraged when his wife learned to use opium that he drank more and more, until the craving for drink fastened itself upon him even as the drug habit had enslaved his wife. Sometimes the man drank until he was drowsy with sleep and cared for nothing else, but he always remembered to keep the key to his money drawer hidden in his clothes lest his wife steal the money.

So desperate did Mrs. Tu become to satisfy her craving that she learned to pick the lock of the drawer where the money was kept. If her husband missed some of his money and accused her of taking it, she would tell him that his son had forced the lock. There were times when the woman became so angry at her husband because she could not have a little cash to ease her distress that she dashed the earthen tea pot to the ground or threw the heavy blue bowls on the earthen floor and broke them.

When the father drank too much, the mother often wept. Then he would send their only child who lived, Huai Sheng, to kneel before the mother and beg her to cool her anger. Whenever the mother smoked her opium pipe and the father saw her, the tears fell from his own eyes, and he sometimes lamented with a loud voice to see all the evil that had befallen them. If the mother could arouse herself from her pleasant dreams enough to hear the cry of grief, she would command the boy to ask his father to stop weeping.

During those days of sadness, the ten-year-old son buried his sorrows in his aching heart and told no one, but he learned patience, and he was comforted through the Bible stories which Teacher Chu told in school.

After a few years, the school closed and was not re-opened. The teacher helped in the evangelistic work at an outstation, and the boys were left with nothing to do. Some of them amused themselves by watching idle folk who spent most of their time at the gambling table. In a short time most of them had learned the game and were eager to try a hand at it, but their parents were too poor to permit their sons to spend money in this way. Where they were not allowed to develop their skill openly, the boys stole away to some quiet place outside the town, usually near the burying ground of some well-to-do family where they could hide behind the grave mounds or climb the trees when in danger of being discovered.

A Chinese Barber at Work

One day they climbed so hastily when some of the parents were looking for them that one of the boys left a garment lying under the trees. When the father saw his son's padded coat spread out on the ground, he looked in the limbs above him. Sure enough, the gang were all there, each one sitting on his own bough!

Silver, a young woman evangelist with a heart aflame for God, went to Mulberry Market Town for a station class, and her theme was "The Cross of Christ." One of Huai Sheng's aunts had become a true Christian, and her interest in her nephew caused her to see that he attended those classes. He had gone to government school after the mission school closed and was no longer interested in the things which he had learned at the mission. Although he sat in the chapel and seemed to listen, his mind was thinking of other things far removed from him. The last day of the class, Silver preached on the suffering and death of Christ and she asked, "Why do you still harden your hearts and not repent?"

The boy could no longer sit still. He went out on the street to see if there were not something of interest there, but the sentence spoken by Silver kept ringing in his ears. He could not forget it. Whatever he did, he was unhappy and could feel nothing but sorrow in his heart. He could not stay away so went back to the chapel just as the Christians were ready to kneel in prayer. Before they did so, Silver asked for any who might want to repent to raise his hand. Timidly, Huai Sheng lifted his hand and Evangelist Chu, who had come to the meeting for that day, saw it. He went to the boy and knelt by his side. In tears the lad prayed brokenly a few sentences, and a deep peace filled his heart. He seemed to hear a gentle voice say, "Thy sins are forgiven; sin no more."

The government school opened again, but Tu Huai Sheng had found work at a shop so did not go. Since he was an apprentice, the proprietor furnished his clothes and his food and gave him three dollars in cash each year. The boy gave one of the three dollars to the mission as an offering the first year.

He had to serve those who gambled and used heroin, and he could seldom get permission to attend the services at the mission, but he had written in his Bible his covenant to give himself wholly to God. This helped him at that time, and it has been a source of strength to him down through the years. As he poured tea and waited in the shop until the early morning hours for the men to go, Huai Sheng felt that he could not remain a Christian if he stayed in the place, so he left.

The hot water business at home was not good, and his mother was more of a slave to her opium pipe all the time, getting money in any way that she could. The boy could not stay at home, for there was no food for him. He had to seek employment.

He found work at a store near the mission and was given time to attend the Sunday meetings. Faithful Chang, the gate evangelist, taught him many hymns and gave him wise counsel. The nights were much the same as at the other shop, but there was no other way. Many a night, the boy ground grain all night after working through the day. He had to feed the donkey two or three times during each night, even when it was cold, for the Chinese always get up a few times in the night to feed their beasts. When he overslept and did not give the donkey his chopped straw with a handful of grain in it at the right time, his employer was angry and scolded him.

He ate at the same table with the men, but they ate quickly as business men do, almost swallowing their food whole, while he ate slowly. When the others had finished, he must place his chopsticks across his bowl as though he had eaten sufficiently, for it would never do to have a servant eat longer than his superiors. The boy swept the dirt floor, rinsed the bowls in cold water after the meals, and prepared the food. The proprietor always looked carefully to see just how much food was left in any bowl or in the kettle so that there could be no eating on the side.

While grinding grain at night, there were times when he could hardly keep his eyes open. Although things were so hard, Faithful Chang helped and encouraged him so much that he did not yield to temptation.

The store sold notions, the sales being largely those connected with idol worship. The place was so given over to Satan that the boy felt he could not stay on, neither could he live in such a sinful home as his own. He gave up his work and went to see his aunt. Although she was very poor, she offered to furnish his food until he could find some other work if he could sleep at the mission.

Mr. Chang's son, Joseph, was with his father and attending the government school. The father made the two boys get up early every morning so that there would be time for prayer. They read from the Bible verse about, Mr. Chang explaining the meaning. Then after he prayed, he encouraged the two boys to lead out in prayer. Each day they memorized a stanza of some hymn as they sang it over and over. Huai Sheng helped Mr. Chang with the sweeping and getting the chapel and courtyards in order for the Sunday meetings.

With the coming of spring, the war lords stirred themselves and began moving about the country, for they were preparing to go out to battle. One fine morning when the sky was rosy-hued and the sun just ready to peep out, a handful of grey-coated men on horseback came galloping toward town. They rode down the street asking for the headman of the town. When they had found him, they ordered him to prepare food for hundreds of men. The soldiers turned into an inn and commanded the proprietor to make haste and give them hot water for their faces. While they were washing, the man was scrambling eggs for their breakfast.

Mothers hurried their unmarried daughters and their son's wives, if they were young and attractive, to near-by villages where they hoped the soldiers would not be passing. People who had valuables sought out a good hiding place for them if they could not take them to another town. Some who had silver dollars tore a brick out of the bed and buried the money there. Others hid theirs in the earth-floor and put some leaves or other fuel over it. Or they found places in a wall where a brick was loose.

Feverishly the people worked, making their precious posses-sions as safe as they could, and the women hid themselves in the inner courts behind barred doors where they would be safe if the soldiers did not tarry too long. Some who could do so unobserved by the vanguard, concealed satin and fur garments under the kaoliang stalks spread on the flat roofs of their houses. Others threw their bedding over a wall where some member of the family waited to tie it into a tight roll and carry it on his back to a relative's home in some other town.

No one dared to tidy her home lest the soldiers want to rest there, and many of the people had no desire for food, neither the courage to cook it. There was nothing to do but wait and hope that the army would move on as soon as they had refreshed themselves with hot water and steamed bread.

Strong young men, being afraid that they might be forced to carry loads or act as stretcher-bearers for the wounded, thought of things they could do away from the home town that day. The older men stood at their gates, if they were not too much afraid to have them open, and looked up and down the street to see what they could, listening for any rumor which might be afloat.

Before the sun was hot, hordes of dusty, grey-clad men tramped heavily and in unison as they came pouring in through the north gate of the town. Some of them wore soiled, ragged uniforms, and their faces were coarse and hostile. Many of the men shouldered guns which had sharp knives sticking from one end, and the steel blades glittered and flashed in the sunshine. They marched down the street a short distance. Then they took possession of all the good buildings which they could find. After these were filled, they streamed into poorer homes so that almost every family had a few uninvited guests.

The general was looking for recruits, for he wanted to enlarge his army. He had a number of young lads who acted as servants to some of the officers until they were old enough to learn to fight. Their marching about over the country was training them to endure hardship. He would take boys of almost any age if they could keep up on the road. Some of the parents were so poor that they were willing for their boys to enlist with this leader.

Mr. Tu had gone into tuberculosis because of his drinking.

He could no longer make a living. Mrs. Tu had become such an opium fiend that she ate the pills when she could buy or steal them. Driven to desperation, they sold Huai Sheng, their only son, to be a soldier.

The officers came to look the sixteen-year-old boy over as if they were buying a horse. When they had finished, they promised to give the parents three hundred dollars the day they left when their son would be expected to go with them.

One morning the word was passed around for all to prepare to march. Huai Sheng did not want to be a soldier. He fled to a field some distance from town where he hid all day long by an old tree stump. When he felt quite sure that the men had all left the town, he returned to the mission.

Next, the parents arranged with a Taoist temple for their son to become a priest. There was to be no salary the first two or three years during his novitiate, but he would be given food and clothing. After that there would be money for his parents, according to his ability to earn it. Faithful Chang and others took this boy's problem upon their hearts and again God heard prayer. The father was growing worse rapidly, and he decided to keep his boy at home until a change came for the better before sending him to abide at the temple, for the son could never come home to live after he had become a novice.

Huai Sheng still ate with his aunt for there was no food at home. Neither was there any money. The boy often took a crude basket on his arm and went out with a manure fork. When he had collected enough of the fertilizer from the road side to fill his basket, he sold it and bought food for his sick father. He did everything that he could to win his father to the Lord, but the man would not seek salvation. He was more troubled because there was no coffin for the burial of his body than he was about a place for his soul.

After Mr. Tu died, his wife sold the table and the chairs from the home to buy opium. The Christian aunt helped Huai Sheng and they locked the mother into a room where no one else could see her. The aunt took food from her own scant store, though she could not afford to do it. She fed the woman for many days, hoping to cure her craving for opium. There was an outside gate to the courtyard and some evil-doers who also used opium slipped into the yard at night and put a little opium under the door. There seemed to be no use to do more unless the woman wanted to have her chains broken, so they set her free and she went to the country to visit a relative.

While he was an apprentice, Huai Sheng wore good clothing, for the shop wanted him to look well. He had warm, padded garments and heavy socks for the winter. His mother offered to rip the clothing out and wash it. Then she would sew it together again, she said. Not knowing what else to do, the boy gladly accepted her offer. As soon as the clothes were ready for wear, the mother tied them in a bundle and carried them to a pawn shop, and she took the socks and the heavy quilt along, for she must have more opium. Some days had passed before the son knew what had happened. When he went home to get his quilt and his warmer clothes he could not find them, and his mother lay in a stupor.

After he found out where the clothes were, Evangelist Small-gate went to see what could be done, but the pawnbroker had already sold the clothes, for he knew that Mrs. Tu would never redeem them. As Faithful Chang and the boy prayed together, his heart was comforted for he felt that God could not forsake one who had no way before him.

The Christians were much interested in Huai Sheng and felt that he was a willing lad and one who would succeed if he had half a chance. A missionary asked him to work one hour each day at any task there was to do and to spend the rest of his time in school. In exchange for his work she gave him a small allowance which was enough to buy his food, for the aunt could not continue sharing for an indefinite period the little that she had.

After three semesters, Huai Sheng graduated from the government school. He made a beautiful picture for the missionary and gave it to her for a present. She asked him to make more pictures, and she sent them to America, secretly hoping that they could be sold for enough to help the boy take more training. Of course he did not know of her plan.

After school closed there was a special class at Tungchangfu for volunteer workers, and Tu Huai Sheng attended it. His heart was happy, and he felt that he should trust God to open a way for him to take training for Christian work. He prayed a great deal and asked the Lord to show him clearly if he should be a preacher. If this was God's plan for his life, he asked that the big ditch back of the chapel be filled with rain. While he prayed the rain began to fall, and it continued until the ditch was full to overflowing. Like Gideon he was afraid to stop when one sign had been given, so he prayed until he saw two more. Then he thought of Moses as he tried to be excused for his lack of eloquence and slowness of speech.

The boy claimed as a promise for himself those words in Exodus 4:12: "Now therefore go, and I will be with thy mouth, and teach thee what thou shalt say."

Huai Sheng earned enough money from his pictures for the first term of school during the summer, but there was no money for clothing. Some of the Christians bought cloth, and others sewed for him so that he was ready to go when the time came.

Whenever he needed new socks, shoes, and things for which he had no money, he did not tell any one, but he prayed about it. He kept a prayer book and each time that he asked God for something, he wrote about it in that little book. When the answer came he recorded the date in the book.

While attending school in Tientsin, his first practical work was at a government hospital. Every Sunday afternoon they gave out tracts and pictures as they went from bed to bed, dealing personally with the patients. The head of the hospital was glad for them to work among the sick folk as it had a good effect upon them. If a hard rain kept the students away, the patients would say that they had missed them as much as children did their parents. One person preached to those who could get about by themselves. More than sixty persons became inquirers that first term.

The second term of school, Tu Huai Sheng was appointed to visit a yard where carpenters and blacksmiths worked. There were always more than one dozen men, and during busy times they added a number of extra workers. Some forty people repented during the four months through the weekly visits and meetings.

Just before his graduation in 1937, Tu Huai Sheng wrote the following testimony:

"I glory in my infirmities and in the cross of Christ. It has been a joy to me to be here in school these three years. I have had the sweetest and most intimate fellowship with my Lord. Sometimes while I am talking to Him for a half hour, or even for an hour or two, He gives me the special help and strength which I need. There are times when I pray silently with the tears running down my face and my heart filled with sweet communion. What do I pray about? When I see my country-men in heathen darkness, going into eternity without God, and when I look upon the sorrows of my people, I can but pray for them. Jesus is the potter, and I am the clay. I desire that He shall mold me after His own will."

After returning to Shantung, Mr. Tu preached at an out-station for two years. During that period, he became engaged to the younger of the Li sisters, Bright Moon. While a young girl of seven she first heard the gospel and her mother became a Christian. Two years later she was converted at Sunday School. From that time the little girl felt that she must reach those who had never heard. Her mother became a Bible woman, and Bright Moon attended our girls' school at Tung-changfu, graduating from high school at the age of seventeen.

Afterwards Miss Li taught in one of the schools for more than two years and did evangelistic work for a few years until the way opened for her to attend the Tientsin Seminary. She knew that she was to give her whole life to the high and holy calling of soul winning, so was very happy that she could prepare herself for her work. Her life was a blessing to all the other students, and she stood at the head of her class. She was a faithful, earnest, prayerful worker in the school, and she has continued to grow and to throw her whole soul into her work. She has become a splendid preacher and personal worker.

Bright Moon and Huai Sheng were married soon after their engagement, and she taught in the Short Term Bible School and did evangelistic work between times. Tu Huai Sheng, having less education than his wife, attended a Seminary at Tenghsien for two years. Then he stayed out of school for a time to gain further experience in evangelistic work, hoping to return to the school for his last year. But such changes have taken place in China that he can make no plans.

Not only are the Tus good preachers and capable workers, but they have established a real home. They keep their house clean and attractive and flowers bloom at their curtained windows. Their little courtyard is filled with shrubs and bright blossoms, too, even though Mr. Tu had to carry water quite a distance to make his plants grow.

Splendid Glory, born in the summer of 1941, is kept sweet and clean, and she is as carefully trained as a missionary's child. Through the winter and spring she slept while her parents were at Sunday School and church. If she awakened before they returned she lay in her crib and played with her toys until she heard the key turn in the door.

Mrs. Tu has a splendid Sunday School for the children which is attended by about one hundred and fifty children every Sunday, and many of these children are real Christians. Near Christmas there are sometimes three or four hundred children.

She has trained young girls to teach the classes, and nine girls volunteer for this service each Sunday.

Mrs. Tu has used her tithe to help poor Christians. Not a few discouraged souls have been given a lift, also some words of encouragement, just when they needed them most. She has kept unceasingly at her task and is always on the alert to help any one she can—any little child who is meeting opposition at home or at school, or any old woman, no matter how stupid. She is dearly loved by all who come in contact with her.

Although their support must now come entirely from the Chinese Christians, the Tu family have no thought of turning aside to other work, for they feel that their needs will be supplied as they go forward serving and trusting the God who has never failed His own.

M RS. LIU AROSE early on Sunday morning for it was
the fifteenth of the moon, and she planned to go to
the mission at Mulberry Market Town (Sangachen) with some
of the women of her village.

Mr. Liu and the thirteen-year-old son had set up a stall at
the market where they sold cheap food until the famine came.
They heard the Jesus doctrine at the street chapel at Mulberry
Market Town, and both of them became inquirers. There
had been no wheat crop that year and the mission gave out
famine relief money. Mr. Liu spent the two pieces of silver
which the missionary gave him for grain. His family ground
this grain between two heavy stones, mixing the meal with
tender leaves and young sprouts to make it last longer. In
this way they were kept alive until the summer crops could
be harvested. The ground was moist enough that autumn to
sprout the precious kernels of wheat which were planted in
the fine yellow soil, and now there was the promise of an
abundant crop.

The mother lifted the two hens from their basket under the
table and turned them loose in the yard. Then she went into
the inner room and brought a handful of kaoliang grains
which she threw into the court for the chickens. Afterwards
she went to the earthen stove and, squatting on her little feet,
lighted a bunch of dry leaves, blowing the tiny flame carefully

as she added more of the leaves, a few at a time, until the fire roared under the iron cauldron.

When the water in the big kettle began to steam, the mother dipped some of it into a basin for her husband and son to wash their faces. After the father had emptied his two large pails of water into the big earthen jar that stood just inside the kitchen door, he took the carrying pole and heavy wooden buckets outside and noisily set them down.

Mr. Liu came back into the room and loosened his garment so that he could wash more thoroughly. He reached for the dingy towel hanging on a peg in the mud wall, dipped it into the steaming water, and held it to his lean face. The girl finished sweeping the dirt floor, brushing the fine particles of earth into a big reed dustpan which she carried outside to empty. After the father had washed to his satisfaction, the rest of the family used the same water, for fuel was too precious to heat water separately for each one.

Mrs. Liu had promised Prosperity Abundant that she might accompany her to the mission that day, although the little girl was only seven and the road was long—fifteen li even when one took the short-cuts through the plowed fields instead of following the big cart road. The child was so full of excitement that she awakened as soon as she heard her mother moving about in the room. She opened her dainty pink mouth and yawned softly a few times, then she scampered out of bed.

When the simple meal was over the father and son wrapped their New Testaments and song books in pieces of cloth and started for the mission. They wanted to arrive early so that the gate-evangelist could teach them another song before the people gathered for the meetings. Mr. Liu did not put much stress on tunes, usually making the words fit his own melody, but the lad, having a quick ear and a retentive memory, sang the songs exactly as the one who taught him. There might be time to learn a few more characters, too, if they walked rapidly, but they remembered that this was a market day, and there would probably be no time for study.

The twelve-year-old girl rinsed the coarse chopsticks and the blue and white bowls with cold water. Then she stacked them into the crude cupboard that was built in the wall.

After the mother pulled the rough, wooden comb through her hair a few times, she twisted a firm knot at the back of her neck and put a silver-washed pin through it to hold it in place. She brushed the hair from her shoulders, wadded the combings into a little knot and poked them into a hole in the wall. Then she combed Prosperity Abundant's little pigtail, braiding a long string of bright red yarn into the hair and wrapping it around the braid several times before tying it near the end. The little girl put on her pretty flowered jacket which was lined, for it was made for fall and spring wear and was not so warm as the wadded one she had worn during the winter. She turned to her sister who fastened the tiny twisted buttons for her. Then the sister smoothed the long straight bangs across the child's forehead.

By this time the two little sisters of four and two were wide awake and clamoring to be dressed. Big Sister helped them into their pretty, seatless trousers and small coats. The mother hurried to don her own clean blue garment which had been freshly washed in the pool the day before and ironed by

77

pounding it while still damp on the big flat ironing-stone out-side the door. The coat was big enough to cover the soiled garment which she wore underneath it.

When the wee girls saw that Prosperity Abundant was going with their mother they set up a howl to go along. The mother showed them the ten eggs which she had carefully saved and tied in a faded blue cloth. She soothed them by saying, "You could never walk so far, and I do not have strength to carry two children. When I have sold these eggs I'll buy some sweets for you. You may go with me when you are somewhat older." She dried their tears with the palm of her hand and gave each of them a copper coin, and thus they were comforted.

Just then the dog growled fiercely and ran toward the big gate, barking as he ran. Mrs. Wang called out in her hearty way, "Have you eaten, Cousin? Then we should be on our way for the road is long."

"Aye! I am ready. Let's be off!"

The three women and the child started out, the women all chattering at the same time and the child too happy for words. The day was cloudless and full of sunshine. The women re-joiced over the good crops growing in the fields and because there was neither war lord nor bandit band in their section of the country that spring.

The child was happy. She was going to the mission for the first time and she could see the market on her way. She had gone to a Catholic Church near her village a number of times, but she had not learned any pretty songs there like her brother learned at the mission. She had been baptized and given her name by the priest. She was proud to have a name for most little girls did not have names. Her two younger sisters did not. Her brother called them "Third Younger Sister" and "Fourth Younger Sister." Sometimes he called Prosperity Abundant by her name and sometimes he called her "Second

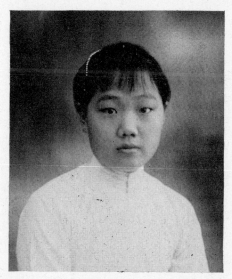

Miss Liu, R. N.

Younger Sister." Her father had hoped that the priest would help him in his quarrels but, after being a member of the church for four whole years, he was so disappointed that he left the Catholics.

The lively girl caught a pretty butterfly by its wings and held it fast in her chubby hand. She heard a whistling sound above her and looked up to see a blue-winged pigeon flying over her head. She had watched her brother fasten a whistle in the feathers of a white pigeon once, and it sounded just like this one did when he set it free. A group of boys near one of the villages through which they passed were holding long cords in their hands. High in the sky above them floated two beautiful kites, proudly flaunting their long tails after them.

Slight gusts of wind sprang up suddenly now and then sending the full-blown white blossoms of the pear trees drifting here and there. The willow trees which grew along the ponds outside the village walls were green with fresh new leaves. A gentle breeze stirred in the wheat fields, bending the long green blades in ripples like waves on a small lake until it softly died away.

During the early days of spring the farmers hauled heaping loads of manure out to their fields in lumbering ox carts. There they heaped it in mounds like the numberless graves that dotted the country-side, only the mounds were smaller than the graves. Today some of the men were scattering these little mounds over their fields. Others were plowing with an ox or a donkey, or perhaps both yoked together.

Prosperity Abundant's sturdy legs ached, and the women were tired. They sat down to rest a bit under a spreading tree. The tree was old and gnarled, and it was in the temple yard near the north gate of the market town. On hot summer days this tree made a cool shade, but its leaves were not fully grown yet. People said that there was a spirit in the tree, and some people worshipped that spirit.

A beggar huddled up against the door of the little temple where he sat in the warm sunshine, carefully examining the seams of his tattered coat which he had just taken off. With his few scattered teeth he bit off the head of every louse that he found in his garment. When he had finished his search he put the old, filthy coat on again. Groaning feebly, for he was dried and wrinkled with age and poverty, he reached a trembling, claw-like hand for his crooked old stick and leaned heavily on it as he hobbled off toward the market.

Bare-backed, sun-browned men, dripping sweat from every pore, passed by. They were pushing great loads of grain, or coal, or pottery on their ungreased, squeaking wheelbarrows. Some had carrying-poles over their muscular shoulders with heavy loads swinging from both ends of the poles. Others walked together in clusters, chatting of one thing and another. Some of them carried a few eggs to sell or a hen which no longer laid enough to pay for her feed. A few of the people rode stumbling little donkeys with tiny, tinkling bells on their necks.

Grandma Li arose to her feet and shaded her eyes with her hands as she squinted at the sun to judge the time of day. As she looked she exclaimed, "It is time for us to be moving on if Prosperity Abundant's mother wants to sell those eggs before she goes to meeting. Anyone can see that she has not been to the mission many times, or she would know better than to take eggs to sell at the market on Sunday. Christians should neither buy nor sell on the holy day of worship."

The streets were full of people, some going south and others coming north. The women could hardly squeeze their way though. They must go to the south end of the long street, for that was where the mission was located. The egg market being near the north end of the street, Mrs. Liu quickly disposed of her precious little bundle lest some one press against her and break the eggs.

The boards had been removed from the fronts of most of the shops along the main street where the market was held, and any one could see at a single glance just what was sold inside. Besides, each shop had a board covered with huge Chinese characters, placed in a conspicuous place where all who could read might see from a long distance.

Vegetable sellers were scattered along both sides of the street. One could buy spinach, curling bean sprouts, bunches of green onions, leeks and garlic. Some carried baskets on their arms from which they sold peanuts and cigarettes. Grain sellers stood beside their wheelbarrows as they measured the grain with wooden, box-like measures. Cloth sellers spread their cloth on tiny tables where all could see, and many a person stopped to feel a piece and ask the price. There were baby chicks for sale, also full-grown roosters and laying hens. One man carried a large bunch of long feather dusters in his arms, and there was another man selling incense and paper money to use in idol worship.

Pieces of pork and beef, looking none too fresh, hung from poles where passers-by must take care if they did not wish to rub their clothing against them. Flies were swarming about, and the dust from the tramping of hundreds of cloth-shod feet arose and settled on the meat. Thin, mangy dogs hovered around, waiting patiently to lick up any drop of blood which chanced to fall.

Footsore and weary, the women hobbled into the women's

side of the chapel. They nodded cheerfully, right and left, to those they happened to know, before they seated themselves on long, backless benches. Some of the benches were sagged in the middle from having held too many people so many times. When the women were wearing padded clothes, five

Market Day at Mulberry Market Town

of them could crowd together on one bench. When they wore less clothing, six women could sit on one seat if the crowd happened to be large.

When the long service was ended the women went to the gate house in the court for women. Here they sat on other narrow, backless benches, but these were shorter than those in the chapel. They drank hot water and talked about the crops and the prices at the market. After a time, Mrs. Liu cleared her throat very loudly and spat upon the brick floor. Then she rubbed the place clean with the quilted sole of her cotton shoe as she said, "We'd better be starting our bodies on the homeward journey, for I must buy something for the two little slaves at home. Prosperity Abundant is too tired to hurry, and we want to get home before the sun lowers."

"You have spoken rightly," joined the others, "let's go."

The women walked single file across the courtyard and through the big gate, bowing their heads to first one and another and calling out as they went, "Tsai chien (see you again)!"

The spring days passed quickly. Soon the wheat fields were golden with the ripening grain. Prosperity Abundant and her four-year-old sister spent most of each day sitting along the edge of the field where they could see any who passed. There were always those who would snatch a few handfuls of the well-filled sheaves when no one was looking. Occasionally the children threw a pebble at a crow or some other bird. Before the wheat was fully ripe, the harvest bird came and sang his glad song.

The day that Mr. Liu and his son cut the wheat with tiny hand sickles, Mrs. Liu and Prosperity Abundant went out to help pile the sheaves in ricks so that they would be ready to load on the ox cart and haul to the threshing floor in front of the house. Big Sister stayed at home to look after the house. She kept her eye on the threshing floor, too. Droves of poor women and children followed the reapers. They went over the short stubble, foot by foot, gleaning a wheat head here and another there, content if only they had a few handfuls at the close of the long, wearisome day.

While the father was heaping the wheat on the threshing-floor that it might ripen more thoroughly, the boy and his mother turned the stubbly ground with their hoes, digging up every single root and saving it for fuel. After the wheat had been pounded out with flails and winnowed to remove the chaff, it was stored in great wicker containers which had been plastered with mud to keep the grain from sifting out. The straw was neatly stacked in a corner of the outer court and a mud roof spread over it to keep out the summer rains. Seeing that the seventeen mu of poor land would hardly support the family even during the good years, the brother learned to mend broken teapots and bowls. He bored tiny holes along both sides of the cracks and fastened the pieces together with strong brass rivets set across the seams. Mr. Liu went with the lad to the markets and helped as he could, but his fingers were never nimble like those of his clever son.

When not busy at their trade, they worked on the land. Mrs. Liu often went to the field to help hoe the growing corn or soybeans. Every spare moment she was spinning thread or weaving cloth on her crude, handmade loom. The oldest girl was getting to be a great help with the sewing. She was learning to weave, too, but she was not so expert at it as her mother.

Two years after Prosperity Abundant went with her mother to Mulberry Market Town, another baby sister was born Five girls! The neighbors wondered, and so did the parents, how they would ever find husbands for all of them. But husbands they must have, for no one ever thought of remaining single in those days. It looked like they had better begin at once, so a match-maker found a husband for Big Sister. She was married the next summer when she was only fifteen.

That was a hot summer, and the flies were worse than common. When Mr. Liu saw that the wheat crop would be scant, he planted a patch of watermelons. He carried large pails of water to keep the vines alive, for it was a dry summer. He caught the bugs from the vines and crushed them in his hands. Before the melons were ripe, he began taking them to market at different towns. He would slice some of the melons and lay the pieces in a big shallow basket where any who passed might see their red or yellow juiciness and be tempted to buy. The left-over pieces which no one would buy he took home at night for his wife and children to eat.

One sultry night after Mrs. Liu had eaten freely of the left-over slices of melon, violent vomiting and purging seized her, and griping pains tore at her vitals. The dignified, be-spectacled, and wise-looking doctor came with his medicines and needles. After feeling of both wrists, the physician said that puncturing with needles was the only remedy. The malady was cholera! The woman writhed in pain through the next day and moaned incessantly. She was not able to eat anything, and her illness made her weak. The next morning she died.

The newly-wed sister took the year-old baby to her mother-in-law's home. There she cared for it as though it had been her own child. Women relatives made the shoes and other garments, and Prosperity Abundant did the cooking as well as a little ten-year-old girl could. She was not really ten, either, for the Chinese way of counting makes one a year older than ʒe actually is.

Scorching winds blew day after day, and the crops turned yellow from the lack of rain. Naked boys cooled themselves in the filthy pools until the slimy water disappeared into the cracked ground. Incense smoked at every little wayside shrine, and women and men prostrated themselves before the temple gods.

There were rain processions in which all but the Christians took part. Some of the more important gods were brought from their cool and shady places in the temples and carried through the stifling, dusty streets, out to the edges of the village so that they could behold the parched earth for themselves. The people left these gods sitting in the blazing sun all day long so that they might feel the heat upon their own heads, hoping that their wooden hearts might be moved to pity those who worshipped them. But the gods had no compassion, and the brassy skies never yielded more than a sprinkle of rain.

In spite of large stretches of sandy waste land, the population of Shantung Province averaged nearly seven hundred people for each square mile, so there was a famine in some part of the province almost every year. There was never much surplus grain even during the good years; but there were places where the harvest was bountiful that year, and the people would have shared their grain for good silver had there been a railroad or a waterway in the section around Mulberry Market Town.

Famine settled down like a great black cloud over the people. Anyone who owned an ox, a donkey, or a cart sold it. Those who had money hidden away in a wall or buried in the earth took it out and bought grain while it could be obtained. People began selling benches and tables, and some even lifted the doors from their hinges and bartered them for food. Some who had a room that could be spared tore it down and sold the timbers and bricks used in the foundation.

The poor searched the fields, gleaning anything that they could find to stay their hunger or use for fuel. Unscrupulous men came from other parts of the country to buy children. Many little girls were sold to be wives or slaves in far away Shensi. The parents reasoned that the whole family would starve if they tried to stay together, and that the child would have to be some one's wife, anyway, before many years. Of course, they wept when they parted from their daughters. They would probably never meet again.

Men who were real Christians would not sell their wives nor their children. Some of them went to other places to seek for work. Others went out to beg if they were too old to work and no other way opened before them. Since Mr. Liu was not well established in the Christian teaching, the evangelist feared that he might be tempted to sell Prosperity Abundant or one of her younger sisters, and he told the missionary of his anxious concern. A missionary offered to support Prosperity Abundant in school, knowing that she would be safe there. The father would hardly dare sell one of the other girls after accepting such an offer as this. Besides he really loved his girls and did not want to part with even one of them.

How happy the little girl was when her father took her to school! His pocket was almost empty, but he fumbled in his girdle until he found two or three copper coins which he put into her chubby hand before he left her. He swallowed hard, but the lump stayed in his throat.

"Be a good girl," he said, "and study diligently, for this is your opportunity to obtain learning. Don't worry about us at home. We will get along some way. Don't let yourself get homesick." Mr. Liu turned and slowly walked away.

Prosperity Abundant was a bright, lovable child, and she advanced rapidly. Besides her school curriculum she learned to tat. After two or three years she could make such dainty, even rings that she could pay her way in school with her tatting shuttle.

During those first few years she sought every time there was a revival in the school, but she was never really converted. The older girls led some of the meetings, and one of them informed her schoolmates that the Jews were all returning to Palestine, therefore Jesus would come back to earth soon. Prosperity Abundant went into a room alone and wept and prayed. Peace came to her heart. She was so careful after that not to quarrel with the other girls. She did want to be good and go up in the Rapture.

A girl whose name was Beautiful Jade led a meeting soon after that. She exhorted the others to read their Bibles and pray every day. Prosperity Abundant did not agree with this leader. She gave her own views to a group of the younger girls as they stood together in the sunshine at the noon hour.

"We do not have to read the Bible and pray every single

89

day! When we read a lot one day it is all right to skip the next, or even several days."

Some made one hundred per cent in their examinations, and they did not study half as hard as Prosperity Abundant. She decided that she would try their method the very next time she had a test. She put the book in her desk drawer and left the drawer open just enough to take a peep when the teacher was not looking. As Teacher Li sat at his desk, peering over his horn spectacles, and stroking his thin, grey beard, he noticed a guilty look overshadow one little girl's face. He arose and leisurely walked to the back of the room where he could get a better view. Sure enough, the girl was cheating! When the teacher went to her desk and took the book away she was dreadfully frightened. She felt that she had lost face before her class.

If there was food at home, Prosperity Abundant went home for the New Year vacation. When she was fourteen she spent one month at home at this season of the year. According to the custom she called on a few of the neighbors. They asked her to sing some of the mission hymns for them, and when she complied with their request, there were some scoffers present who ridiculed her religion. When she could stand no more of their gibes, she called out, pretending that she was answering some one, "Yes, I'm coming!" Then she jumped up and hurried quickly from the room, excusing herself by saying, "They want me at home."

Most of the neighbors gambled during their holidays. The men sat around tables, often out in the open streets, while the women generally gathered in a courtyard or at some friend's home. Etiquette demanded that Prosperity Abundant return the calls of relatives and friends. Sometimes she found the women sitting at the game table. She had learned how to handle cards herself before she went to school. She did not see what harm there was in watching the women play. Almost before she realized what she was doing, she was persuaded to join them.

Her heart was always filled with remorse after such occasions, for she knew that she had done wrong. She was afraid of the Day of Judgment and afraid to take her stand as a Christian before those heathen people. Sometimes she lay awake at night and blamed God for creating her with a soul. She did not see why He had not made her a cat, a dog, or a bird—something that did not have a precious soul that could never die! How hard it all seemed. Yes, it was hard to live for God. It was hard to be good, to develop a virtuous character, hard to sing and hard to preach. At school, at home, no peace. What an arduous road it was.

When the morning prayer bell rang the girls were expected to find a quiet place and spend the time with their Bibles or in prayer. One morning Prosperity Abundant heard the quick steps of leather-shod feet. She and another little girl were not observing the quiet hour. They ran inside and knelt as quickly as they could, but not before the missionary had seen them. The girls did not realize how wrong this was at the time. Prosperity Abundant wondered why she couldn't be good and why God ever made a heaven and a hell in the first place.

One day as she prayed alone in the assembly room she saw

a vision of two roads. One of the roads was so narrow that one foot had to be placed before the other to travel it. The broad road ran in another direction with a downhill slope which made it easy to follow. As she beheld the roads a gentle voice spoke to her saying, "Yes, my child, the narrow way is very difficult, but not impossible for you. Death waits for every person. 'And it is appointed unto men once to die but after this the judgment.' "

Never could she forget those solemn words. It was the spring of 1927. The missionaries had been ordered to the coast that they might be protected from the nationalists who were sweeping the land as a raging, destructive fire. At Nanking foreign houses had been looted and some burned. Some foreigners were killed and a number wounded.

Pastor Snow of the China Inland Mission visited different mission stations to encourage the Christians and prepare them for the storm. Prosperity Abundant attended one week of these meetings. She was so afraid that she might disobey God, and she did not know how to please Him. Silver, who was one of her teachers, helped her pray that week. She confessed her sins and made restitution, and God gave her the assurance that she was really born again. From that time on her prayers were answered, and she read her Bible with relish.

When Prosperity Abundant was sixteen, a heathen girl of eighteen years was brought into the home to be the wife of her brother. She felt that she should obey this girl since the Bible tells us to be subject to those over us. But she was determined that she would not work on Sunday nor do things that were wrong.

In the fall of 1927 conditions seemed to be a little better. Some of the missionaries received permission to return to their work, provided they would leave again if notified to do so. The girls' school was moved to Nankwantao. Hard times again visited the people, and more children were sold before the year was over. Prosperity Abundant was fully supporting herself in school, and her heart yearned over the two younger sisters at home. Her father had already engaged her to an evangelist's son, and there was no telling when he might engage her fourteen-year-old sister. Unless she had some schooling it would not be easy to find a Christian home for her. One day Prosperity Abundant came to me, blinking hard to keep back the tears. Her chin quivered until she could hardly speak.

"I know that my folk do not have enough to eat at home," said she. "My next sister wants to come to school so much that she is willing to do anything. I have been teaching her to tat during vacations. I am sure that she can soon earn most of her expenses. I'll work as hard as I possibly can, and I'll help her."

"But you must have time for study," I reminded her.

"If we do not earn enough during the year, I'll tat and do needle work at home next summer. She is trying to be a Christian, but my father does not understand, and my brother's wife is a heathen. If she could be here and learn to read the Bible she would be stronger when temptations come. Oh, please do let her come. The others will have more to eat if there is one less mouth to feed at home."

In less than one week, Little Sister arrived at the school.

Her only baggage was a coarse wooden comb, for she wore all of her clothes. She would have to share her sister's bedding, but her beaming face revealed her happiness.

Prosperity Abundant was distressed that her father did not make greater progress in his Christian life. Sometimes she wondered whether he had ever really been converted. So anxious was she for his salvation that she often went to the prayer room and pleaded for her father while the others were enjoying a meal of millet porridge and dark steamed bread.

After graduating from the girls' school that spring, Prosperity Abundant entered the Tungchangfu Bible School the next fall. Because regulations under the new regime were such that we did not feel it right to comply with them, none of our schools opened for the spring term. It was a big disappointment to the girl to have to return to her home and be under the control of one so young, and a heathen at that. When the opportunity came to teach a village school one hundred li from home, she gladly accepted. She ripped her bedding and washed it so that it would be fresh and clean as a teacher's should be. Before she could go robber bands poured into the country like a flood, killing, looting, burning homes, and taking people for hostages.

The next two and one-half years, Prosperity Abundant worked in a hospital at a neighboring mission. She was so capable and served with such a willing heart that the missionary who was head nurse in the hospital wanted her to really train for a nurse and offered to help her do this. After spending three years at Kaichou she was graduated as a trained nurse. From the time she began earning a salary one ambition possessed her—to take further training at the Peking Union Medical College so that she could become a head nurse and earn more money. The boy to whom she was engaged was not turning out as well as could be hoped. She secretly longed to be free from him but could not honorably break the engagement.

There were times when Nurse Liu felt that she wanted to be wholly surrendered to God and to know that the Holy Spirit filled her heart and completely controlled her life. She was not fully satisfied with her present state and often sought a deeper experience. She felt that she had dedicated her life to God, but there was one thing which troubled her at times —her tithe. Certainly she would give one-tenth of her income to the Lord, but she did not want to give it then. She had other plans for her money. She decided that she would turn over one whole month's pay after she had first used nine for herself. When she saw her mistake, she began to tithe from that day.

There was a growing conviction in her heart that she should go to the Tientsin Bible Seminary and prepare herself more thoroughly for God's work. Just one month from the time that she began to tithe, the head nurse offered to send her to Peking for further training, the hospital paying all the expense. But Miss Liu had given up her own plans and did not want the glory of the world. She turned the offer down. She chose rather to plan for Bible training and to give her life in humble service to Him who deserved all the love of her heart.

When Nurse Liu heard that the Japanese were coming to Tamingfu where she worked, she fled with another young lady nurse to a safer part of the country. They lived in the home of a Christian and did volunteer work for a few months. Then they visited the School of Nursing at Kaichou which was not far away. So many wounded were being brought to the hospital that those in charge were only too glad to add the two nurses to their staff.

Miss Liu had been greatly impressed through the reading of Dr. Sung's testimony. He had stated: "First, a preacher must be sent; second, he must give himself willingly; third, he must not be a preacher because some one helped him in school, or because he can find nothing else to do." There was a *must* in Miss Liu's heart.

Folk thought that Nurse Liu was very foolish to want to go to school again when she was commanding a good salary. Her father was very displeased about it. He had hoped that she would be sending money home regularly and life would be easier for them all. When she tendered her resignation aften ten months of faithful service, the missionary-nurse wept, for she was loathe to give up such a splendid assistant. Miss Liu wept also, but she said, "I *must* go."

In spite of perils of war and perils of robbers, thirty young people, chaperoned by Dr. Troxel, traveled to Tientsin by boat that autumn. Prosperity Abundant was one of them.

While making her adjustments during the first term, she decided that she would not preach about a Spirit-filled life, for it was too hard for folk to reach this state. She did not feel satisfied that she had obtained it herself. Before the second term had ended there was a deep and abiding peace in her heart. She knew that the Comforter had come. A text was impressed upon her mind and she claimed it for her own: "I will make you to become fishers of men." Relying upon Mark 1:17 she led thirteen girls, students like herself, into a deeper experience such as she now enjoyed. Great peace filled her heart and her worries were all gone.

Four or five days before the close of school, Prosperity Abundant spent her last penny, and she had no work for the summer. She needed money for her second year, but her heart was not troubled. She did not know what to do next, but she knew that her Guide would direct her in the path of His own choosing.

She was not surprised when the dean of women said to her a day or so later, "They need another nurse at one of the mission hospitals this summer and would be glad for you to take the place. You may think it over and report to me by tomorrow."

That first summer Miss Liu led Miss Ling, a nurse, to the Lord. When Miss Caffray went to the Tientsin Bible Seminary for a meeting, the nurse had arranged to live at the school so that she could be in every meeting. And in that meeting she fully yielded her life to God.

Dr. Shih, an American trained man, was on the hospital staff. He had lost faith in God, but he could not fail to see the change in Nurse Ling's life. The next summer Miss Liu worked at the hospital again. All summer long, the doctor asked her questions about God and her experience. Miss Caffray was the evangelist in a Tientsin church soon after that and there Dr. Shih was born again. A few months later he went to be with Jesus.

At times the Chang family wanted their son to marry Miss Liu, but she would ask them to wait awhile longer. She could not tie herself to a young man of his type and feel happy about it. Neither did she see how she could break the engagement and keep the respect of the Chinese. She committed the future to God and waited. The very last term of school, the young man died. Now she was free.

Conditions were getting so tense in the summer of 1941 that the missionaries went to Tientsin for the closing of the Bible Seminary and to make plans for the next year. It looked as if all of us might have to leave China soon, and it seemed wise that we meet together for a few days of prayer and consultation. Miss Liu had accepted an invitation to go to Tungchangfu to teach in the Short Term Bible School and to do evangelistic work. Before leaving she came to a group of us who happened to be together just then. Tears filled her eyes and she sobbed aloud.

"I thank you missionaries for coming to China to teach us about Jesus," she said. "Had you not come we should never have known, and there would have been no school such as this where we could be trained to go out and win others. Pray that I may bring forth much fruit as I go out into the harvest field."

It was a joy to work with Miss Liu at Tungchangfu until we were interned December 8, 1941. Since she was supported by American friends her allowance ceased from that time. A number of the outstations invited her to hold station classes for them, the Christians furnishing her food while she was with them. She cared for a few sick people while in the country and received a little money for that. In one way or another her needs were met.

A Japanese pastor assumed responsibility for the Tientsin Bible Seminary when the soldiers wanted to use the buildings for stables. The school has continued these two years. Since the enrollment was less than half of the usual number, some of the buildings were rented for enough money to cover all the running expenses. Miss Liu was invited to go to Tientsin and serve on the faculty. Perhaps at this time she is training others to become "fishers of men."

The little girl who thought that it was so hard to be good and wished that she had been created without a soul, found that God could help her so that she delighted to please Him each day of her life. Prosperity Abundant was made to know that Jesus could so satisfy her heart that her greatest joy was to tell others of His love.

> "I know that the soul is aided
>   Sometimes by the heart's unrest,
> And to grow means often to suffer—
>   But whatever is—is best.
> I know there are no errors,
>   In the great Eternal plan,
> And all things work together
>   For the final good of man.
> And I know when my soul speeds onward,
>   In its grand Eternal quest,
> I shall say as I look back earthward,
>   Whatever is—is best."

M OST OF THE houses in West Honorable Village were earthen ones, but the Wu family had been very prosperous at the time their house was built nearly one hundred years ago. The thick walls were made of strong, even bricks and the curving, picturesque roofs were covered with tiles. The old buildings were still in good condition, excepting the brick floors which had become rough and full of holes, although the original bricks had been replaced more than once.

The Wus had three children, a girl of fifteen who had been engaged for nearly five years to a boy four years younger than herself; a thirteen year old boy, Excellent Gem; and a baby girl who was just beginning to toddle about by herself.

The villagers were agog with excitement when Mrs. Wu gave birth to three children in one day! People had never heard of such a strange thing, and everyone wanted to see the babies. A constant stream of women, accompanied by children of all ages, visited the home from early morning until late at night. Some called again and again to see how the babies did. Each one politely inquired as to the state of the mother's health, and most of them offered some advice pertaining to the care of mothers and new-born babes.

The relatives and close friends brought presents for the mother. Some presented small packages of red sugar or eggs, while others brought rice or vermicelli, since these things are very fitting gifts for one who has just given birth to a child.

The mother sipped fowl's broth and forced herself to eat eggs with rice or vermicelli. She had looked forward to the time when she could have these delicacies, but now that she had them, they had no flavor. She drank thirstily, bowl after bowl, of hot water in which lumps of the dark sugar had first been dissolved. The aunt who had come to help care for the mother was kept very busy preparing the four daily meals which new mothers are supposed to eat. Then the dirt in the bag which each baby wore had to be changed once, at least, every day for fresh dust which must first be sifted and warmed.

Mr. Wu, wanting to be sure that there was no shortage in the egg supply for his wife, went to the market. There was no clock in the house, but when the sun stood high in the sky and cast a straight shadow at the open door, it was time to prepare the noon meal. The daughter bustled about the dark, smoke-blackened kitchen as she dipped cold water from the large earthen jar with an old gourd-dipper and poured it into the big iron kettle. Then she sat on a low bamboo stool before the brick stove and fed corn stalks into the fire. As soon as the steam bubbled out from under the edge of the wooden lid, she lifted the cover. Dipping some of the boiling water, she filled a small pewter teapot which she carried to her mother's room.

The rest of the water Big Sister poured into a larger tea pot which she set on the rickety little table. She put some more water into the kettle, then busied herself mixing corn meal in an earthen crock. After she had kneaded the mixture until she could shape it into cakes with her hands, she lay them,

101

one against the other, in the steamer until it was nearly full. She picked up some sweet potatoes from the pile under the table and washed them carefully, then she placed them beside the cakes and covered the kettle. Again she sat down before the fire, her smooth brow puckered with frowns, for the smoke smarted her eyes until the tears came.

When the bread had steamed until it was nearly done, the girl lifted the heavy steamer and poured a bowl of tiny, canary-colored millet grains into the hot water. Then she replaced the cover on the kettle and left the millet to simmer away. She shooed a hen out of the door and tidied the room by sweeping the ashes and litter from the fuel into the fire under the kettle while she waited for her father to come from the market.

A growing fever seized the mother's body and consumed her strength. She grew weaker every day, and the babies began to wither away until they looked like wizened old men. The doctor came and felt the pulse in both the sick woman's wrists for a long time, and he looked carefully at her tongue. After he had stuck long, coarse needles into her abdomen to drive out the fever, he wrote out a prescription.

As the physician left, Mr. Wu accompanied him to the big gate, bowing him out in the proper manner. Then he went to a shop where herbs and different kinds of powders could be bought. Although he wanted to hasten that his wife might have the medicines more quickly, propriety demanded that he walk leisurely through the streets and not seem hurried, lest he lose his dignity. As he met his neighbors different ones called to him inquiring about his wife and the babes.

They had heard of the fever and knew of the doctor's visit.

"The physician says that the mother of Excellent Gem has been chilled by an evil wind," Mr. Wu informed those who inquired. "I am now on my way to buy medicine, and she will be all right after she has taken it."

When Mr. Wu returned from his errand, the aunt propped a small kettle on two bricks and built a quick fire under it. After the herbs had boiled for a few minutes, she poured the dark brew into a coarse blue bowl and blew into it with her breath until it was cool enough to drink. Then she lifted the sick woman's head from her hard straw pillow and held the bowl to her lips while she gulped down the bitter potion.

Instead of improving, the mother grew so ill that she no longer heard the moaning of her starving babies. She lay in a stupor and took no notice of those who came or went. When the doctor was called again he felt the sick woman's pulse and slowly shook his head, "If the gods will that she leave you what can I do?" he asked.

The children wept as they stood by their mother's side and begged her not to leave them. Through the weary hours of the long night her husband and the aunt watched while she panted for breath. With the coming of the new day, her gaunt body gave a little shudder and her soul left her.

Solemn-faced and wordless, Mr. Wu glided into an adjoining room lest some one see him as he brushed the unbidden tears from his eyes. As soon as he could control himself enough to appear calm and undisturbed, he gave his attention to making plans for the funeral.

There seemed to be no use trying to save the triplets now

that the mother was gone, for there was neither goat nor cow. Probably the babies would not live anyway, even if they should buy a goat or a cow, so why bother with them? Besides, the daughter's mother-in-law was already impatient for the wedding. What could the father and Excellent Gem do with three more babies if they should live?

Soon after the mother's passing, one of the infants stopped breathing. The father brought a piece of old ragged matting to wrap the body in, and the aunt stooped over the other two to see how long they would live. When she had finished looking, she straightened her shoulders and said to him, "There is still a faint flicker of life in both of them, but they will not last many days at the longest. Why not wrap them all together and be done with their moaning? I need to return to my home anyway."

"We may as well do as you have said," answered the father. "One baby is enough for us to care for, and I do not know how we shall get along after the girl is married."

They wrapped the three babies together—the dead one and the two living ones. The bundle was taken to a little temple yard not far from the house. Some earth was thrown over it, but not enough to completely cover the matting or keep the dogs from finding the bodies. Many people did not bother to do even this but just threw the bodies out when their little ones died.

Mr. Wu, being an older man and fond of his family, could not think of bringing a step-mother into the home lest she mistreat his children. Since his daughter was already considered the property of the Wang family, he must try to get along without her. She prepared her wedding clothes during spare time and was married a few months after her mother died.

The baby sister was so clumsy in her padded garments that she could hardly walk about. She was too heavy and awkward to be carried when she wore them, so Excellent Gem took her bunglesome garments off when they went out to play with the other children, and he carried her inside his own padded jacket. The boy missed his mother and felt neglected. When his little sister cried because she wanted her mother, he cried with her, both of the children wailing at the same time, "My mother, ah, I want you! I am so lonely for you."

Excellent Gem grew into a spoiled, boastful lad who was always trying to pick a quarrel. He learned to gamble, but his skill did not increase with his fondness for the game, so he lost heavily. His father sold some of the land to pay off the boy's debts. Then he forbade his spending more money in this way and saw that the lad was safe in bed at night before he dared push the heavy wooden bolt across the door.

Excellent Gem slept on the inner side of the brick bed and pretended to be asleep while he waited for his father's loud snoring to begin. He arranged his heavy, stiff quilt in such a way that it covered the hard pillow and stood up as if his own body were under it. Then he walked softly like a cat as he stepped over his sleeping father. Silently he unbolted the door and stepped out into the cold, moonlight night. After he had cautiously closed the door, he poked his long, slender fingers through the crack and slipped the bolt into place again. He did this many times, and his father never knew that he was gone until he came creeping in one morning near day-break, and more land had to be sold to pay for his losses.

Like four-fifths of the people of China, the Wu family belonged to the farmer class. As the drought of summer turned to autumn, men watched anxiously every time a cloud appeared. Thin, dark little patches sometimes floated across the sky, but before they had grown large enough to give even a sprinkle of rain, they were scattered by the cold, bitter, north-west wind, laden with fine, yellow, desert soil. This dust sometimes filled the air until the bright sun was hidden from view. It covered the faces and clothing of the people as it drifted into their homes and spread itself over their belongings. Folk not only looked like they were made out of the dust of the earth, but they appeared to be returning to it!

The corn dried up on the stalk until there were only a few scattered grains on each stubby ear. The soybean pods were short and not half filled. The father and the son shelled corn and threshed the beans by hand, carefully gathering every bean from the dust. The vines with their leaves and the stalks of corn were piled in a corner of one of the rooms to be used for cooking their food. It was very clear that the meager supply of grain would not be enough to feed three mouths until another harvest. Excellent Gem was now eighteen years old. His uncle and some of the other men who needed work to keep their families from starving planned to go to Shansi, and the boy decided that he would go with them.

Each of the men rolled his quilt tightly and tied it with a square cloth. At night the men wrapped the quilts about them as they slept, and by day they stuck sticks through the bundles and carried them on their shoulders. Their money was barely enough to buy a bit of coarse bread and hot water. This was their fare, day after day, as they tramped the irksome miles over the mountains and through the valleys.

They came to a large town where a business man arranged with the uncle for Excellent Gem to work for him. When they had finished the agreement, the uncle went farther on to seek employment. Every morning after the boy had swept the store and dusted the shelves and counters with a feather duster, he heated water and carried it in a basin to his master. The man dipped a towel into the scalding water and wrung it out. Rubbing it over his smooth face and shaven head, he ordered, "Bring me my breakfast."

When the merchant had noisily eaten and finished sipping his tea, he put on his long silk gown. Shaking and pulling it into place, he buttoned it at the side, and he was ready to receive his customers. Excellent Gem swept the little court at the back of the shop and carried water from the town well. When the day was cold, he took a crock of smoldering charcoal to the shop so that the master might warm his hands before writing his accounts. Since the business was small and there was no need of an assistant, the proprietor kept his own accounts.

Excellent Gem needed warmer garments to keep out the bitter cold, so he watched for an opportunity to speak with his employer. He was not sure just what agreement his uncle had made, but he felt that there should be a few pieces of silver besides his board. He had worked only one-half of the month, but it was sometimes customary for a servant to get his salary in advance when there was special need for it.

The very next morning, Excellent Gem peeped through the crack in the back door. There was no guest in the room. He watched his employer seat himself at a square, black table, push back his long sleeves and reach for the writing materials. He saw him pour a bit of water on the ink-slab and rub the hard stick of ink across the slab. Feeling that the right moment had come, the boy tucked his hands into his long sleeves, stepped quietly into the room, and coughed lightly to attract the attention of his master.

"Please, sir, may I speak one sentence?" stammered Excellent Gem as the man lifted his eyes.

The merchant pointed his camel's hair brush very sharp and fine, ready to touch the paper before he slowly looked up and called out impatiently, "Well, what is it then? Speak!"

The boy colored slightly as he looked down at his worn and ragged trousers. "You can see that my clothes are too thin for this cold climate. May I have my allowance in advance this month so that I can buy some padded garments?"

"How dare you mention money to me?" screamed the man. "There is no money due you! Your uncle sold you to me, and I put the money on his palm—twice as much as you are worth! You will receive your food but nothing more."

The boy sobbed aloud as he turned to leave the room. He knew that his uncle was a bad man, but he did not know that he could be so cruel. The future looked very dark. He could not run away, for he had no money for the journey. Besides it was not safe for one to travel alone. If he could go home, there would be no food for him. There was nothing for him to do but stay where he was and do his best to win his master's favor.

The business man had two wives. The younger one took a fancy to Excellent Gem and tried to entice him. When he refused to listen to her, her love turned to hatred. One day she struck him with a club, screaming in anger, "You can do nothing well. You are not worth the food that you eat. We would do well to be rid of you!"

Hearing the uproar, the husband appeared in the back door of his shop, his face dark and angry, and the woman cried out to him, "This worthless slave from Shantung dares to insult me! Think of one so low as to try to inveigle his master's wife—the dog! Send him to prison at once!"

After Excellent Gem was sent to jail, his owner tried to hire someone to poison him. A man whose home was also in Shantung had become acquainted with the lad while he was a slave. When he heard that the boy had been sent to jail, he went to the keeper and asked for permission to see him. The jailer did not feel that the boy was guilty of a crime, so gave him permission to leave the prison long enough to go with his friend to see an official from Shantung. This official set the boy free and fined his owner. The man was so enraged over the loss of face that he died in a fit of anger not long after that.

In the early spring the uncle returned to West Honorable Village. Excellent Gem's father was worried when he saw that his boy was not with the uncle, but his brother said, "You have no cause for worry, for your son has a very good job. He does not lack for clothes or food—he has everything that he needs."

Refugees began to return to Shantung, and rumors sifted through that Excellent Gem was in jail. The father's heart was apprehensive for his son. He went to a fortune-teller to see what he should do. Later he consulted a witch. She burned incense and bowed before her gods for a long time. Then she said to Mr. Wu, "Your son died long ago! By this time the flesh has rotted from his bones."

The father mourned for many days, for Excellent Gem was his only son, and he would never have another. His thin body grew more shrunken with the passing of the days, and his hands and feet trembled all the time. Big tears rolled down his wrinkled cheeks sometimes without his being conscious of it. He was stunned by his grief.

One afternoon when the fields were green with spring crops tall enough to bend in the sudden gusts of wind, Excellent Gem walked into his father's front gate. The father aroused himself from his nap to see who had come as he heard the sudden sound of voices. He thought that surely a ghost had appeared, for he supposed that his son had been dead for several months.

"Who said that I was dead?" asked the boy roughly. "If the witch told my father that, then I am through with her and the whole lot of them!"

There was a small Catholic church in the village, and Excellent Gem joined it. He told people on the street that there was a heaven and a hell. A Christian woman heard him speaking thus to a group one day. She learned that the boy was disgusted because the leader of the church, a man named Sung, drank so much wine.

"You must believe in Jesus to be saved. Some of the Christians from the Jesus mission are coming to my home for a meeting tomorrow. I'd be happy for you to come and hear them," said the Christian woman.

The boy was there, and he listened very attentively to those who spoke. On Sunday he went to Nankwantao to hear more. That day he asked Pastor Chang to pray with him. He confessed all the sins of his past life, and everyone in the village saw the change in him. His father did not have to bolt the door to keep him from going out to gamble any more. He no longer drank the two bowls of wine that he could drink at one sitting and not become intoxicated. He was through with wine and gambling forever. His father and his neighbors all rejoiced over the change in him.

When there was any work to be done at the mission station at Ch'ai Pu, Excellent Gem gladly volunteered to help. He spent many days at hard work while they rebuilt the mud walls around the church yard and remodeled and enlarged the building. He never missed a Sunday service, and often invited the evangelist to come to his home for a meeting. He began to tithe and walked in the light as fast as it came to him. He prospered in all that he did. He bought cloth and took it to markets farther to the west where there was no cloth and no cotton for sale. He made good profit at this business and gave thirty eight dollars to the mission station at one time—his tithe of the profit made selling cloth.

The heathen neighbors were so interested that they all wanted to help this fine boy locate a good wife. He was so changed that his disposition was meek and patient. Fearing a heathen wife might not show such a kind husband the respect due him and that she might revile one who did not control her with a firm hand, he refused to become engaged to a heathen girl. His old father was eager for the son to marry so that he might see his grandchildren before his death. Excellent Gem consulted with the Christian woman about a wife, then he prayed about it and waited for the Lord to prepare the right one for him.

An elderly Christian woman was much concerned because her little granddaughter's father was about to engage her to an old man. The man promised to become a Christian and to give the father a dowry of four hundred dollars. The child's mother wanted her daughter to marry a Christian so that she would receive better treatment, for the old man promised so easily, the mother felt that he did not mean to keep his promise. When they talked with the girl's grandmother she said, "You cannot trust any of these men."

Excellent Gem's Christian neighbor being there and hearing the conversation, suggested that the girl marry her neighbor boy. His father had sold off land to pay the boy's gambling debts until now there were only ten mu of land which is one and two-thirds acres, according to American reckoning. The neighbor promised to talk to the boy, suggesting that he watch the girl next Sunday to see how she would suit him.

When the Christian woman led the fourteen-year-old girl slowly through the yard that next Sunday morning Excellent Gem was glancing slyly from the corners of his eyes. There were many people in the yard, but none of them knew that the boy was choosing his future wife.

It was only fair that the girl also have an opportunity to know which boy was interested in her, for the Christians like to know something about those to whom they are thinking of being engaged. Because many war refugees were living at the mission compound, the Christian woman also came there for protection. She asked Excellent Gem to bring her some grain from her home and to carry it into the women's court where she stayed. The girl stood just inside the open window of a near-by room, where she could see clearly without being seen herself, as the boy brought the grain into the yard.

Since both were satisfied, the boy sent the girl's parents eighty dollars and planned to pay her expenses in some mission school until she was old enough to be his wife. He bought her some pretty cloth for her school clothes and sent her two bushels of corn the next day so that she would have something to eat while at home.

Excellent Gem bought more coarse, home-spun cloth of the women in his village and again started for a western market. He had been gone only five or six days when his father suddenly sickened and died. The father knew that his son was engaged, and he asked that the girl be brought for him to see before he died, but the word did not reach her in time.

Now that the son was away, it was the duty of the next of kin to take charge of the funeral arrangements, and the closest relative happened to be the uncle. At the funeral, the nearest kinsman is supposed to break the earthen vessel which has seven holes bored into it. These holes represent seven openings of the body which are united as long as there is life but cease to function after death. This rite should be performed by the son who was the rightful heir of the property, but who knew when he would return from that far away place? The uncle was pleased to take charge of affairs, even to the breaking of the earthen vessel. He was glad to take advantage of his nephew and spend money freely, keeping a good amount for himself as the money passed through his sticky hands.

Mats were propped with poles to make an awning in the courts. Professional cooks came from the food shops, wearing their white, greasy and dirt-soiled aprons. There was the smell of delicious food cooking in the great iron cauldrons which had been hired for the occasion. All the tables had been arranged for the guests, but there were not enough so others were borrowed—red and black lacquered, and plain unpainted ones. The uncle moved about in an important manner giving orders in a loud voice and overseeing this detail and that.

Friends and neighbors came to pay their respects to the deceased and to present their gifts of incense sticks and paper money to be burned at the grave. Hearing that great preparation was being made for feasting, some who had never even seen the Wu family before accompanied those who really went to lament. The first day of mourning, one hundred and fifty guests dined in the rooms and courts, the expenses amounting to almost as many dollars as guests. Even the visitors thought that money was being spent too freely, and they spoke among themselves.

"Isn't Excellent Gem betrothed to a girl who lives only three miles away?" questioned a neighbor. "If money is spent like this throughout the period of mourning before the funeral, there will be nothing left. Why can't the girl break the seven-holed vessel and then the property will be theirs?"

When they took word to the Christian woman who had been the go-between for the engagement, she hurried to send for the girl. When the child came to the mission compound, her clothing was so ragged that different ones gave her shoes, stockings, trousers, and even a jacket. As soon as she was dressed in these things, they started for the village.

"Do you know the proper way to kowtow to your elders?" the woman asked. "As soon as we arrive you must bow respectfully before your fiance's relatives—all of those who are older than you yourself."

When the girl admitted that she did not know the right way to kowtow, they stopped right there by the roadside while the woman taught her. As they reached the outskirts of the village, two women came out to meet them and assist in any way that they could. First, they went to the uncle's home where the girl prostrated herself before the uncle and his wife and three other relatives who were her elders. A table had been prepared with incense, and the uncle commanded that the girl bow before it, but the Christian woman spoke quickly and firmly, "I have been the go-between for the two young people. I object to this girl bowing before the gods."

The neighbors flocked to the uncle's courtyard to congratulate him that there was a new bride in the home to assume responsibility for the funeral. Although the uncle was very angry because he could not proceed with his plans, he buried his feelings in his heart and greeted his friends calmly as though he were very pleased that the girl had come.

It is the custom for a new bride or groom to receive a gift from those to whom a kowtow is given for the first time. There were five who each gave the girl one dollar. She had never had so much money before in her life.

After the introductions were over, the maiden was led into a room where she rested a few minutes while she sipped a bowl of hot water. Then she was escorted to the room where the corpse lay. As soon as she entered the big gate which opened into the court, she lifted up her voice and wailed as loudly as she could, "Oh, my father! My dear father!"

She did not weep long, for she was not dressed properly since she still wore her hair in a braid down her back and had black shoes on her feet. The women assisted her to rise, in a fitting manner, as she appeared too grief-stricken to be able to stand without support. They helped her to the k'ang, which is a brick bed, and there she sat while white cloth was sewn to both sides of her shoes, almost entirely covering the black cloth. They put a band of white cloth around one arm, and after her trousers were folded closely about her ankles, white cloth torn into strips was wound around them. Her long hair was combed and twisted like a rope. Then it was corded and tied with a coarse white string and knotted at the back of her neck. She had no hair pins of her own, but each of the three women who assisted her took one from her own hair.

The girl took her place at the right side of the coffin near the head of it. Here she sat with bowed head and downcast eyes. Each time anyone came to pay his respects to the dead, he wept as he drew near the door and the bride burst into fresh weeping at the same time. She wailed loud and long during the next three days and very little money was spent, while everyone admired and praised her for her filial respect.

At the funeral, the bride leaned on the arm of her uncle's wife and walked before the coffin. She carried the vessel with the seven holes in one hand and the soul-flag, made of very thin, silk-like paper, in the other. When demons came to chase the soul it was to take refuge in the folds of this flag.

All along the narrow street through which the bier passed, incense smoldered away to keep evil spirits from entering the homes. As they reached the street, the girl dashed the earthen vessel to the ground, and she did it so well that it broke into many pieces just as it should. Every few steps, she knelt before the coffin which had a white rooster tied on top of it to call the soul to follow, and she bowed with her forehead touching the ground to thank the pall-bearers for their kindness and hard work. When the coffin was lowered into the grave, she threw three handfuls of earth into the open grave as the son should have done had he been present. She did not bow three times to the gods and four times to the devils as the custom was, because the Christian woman did not wish it. Lamenting loudly, she walked around the grave three times after it had been filled with earth. Thus she showed the sign of separation from the dead.

What should the maid do next? If she went home, more money would have to be spent when Excellent Gem brought her to his home, for there would have to be more feasting. She could not enter another home wearing white patches of cloth sewed to her shoes as they were now, lest there be a death in that home, and it takes time to make new shoes.

The Christian woman decided to stay at home for a few days and take the girl to her own home while they waited for the boy to return so that they could consult with him. When they returned from meeting the next Sunday, they found that he had come home.

Excellent Gem had met with good fortune on his trip and he brought some cakes and some meat for his father. As he came along the street singing lustily, some one called to him, "Stop singing. It is time to weep!"

Quickly looking about to see if there was some one to pick up his things and take care of them, he threw them to the ground and began to wail. His grief was genuine, not only for sorrow at his father's death when he could not be at home to care for him, but because he feared that his uncle had spent everything for the funeral.

After permitting him to weep a short time, his friends followed him to the grave and exhorted him to cease lamenting. They told him that his property was safe, and then they complimented him because he had chosen such a wise and capable girl to be his wife.

The next morning, the bride and her friends and the groom and his, in two groups, far enough apart not to see each other, went to the mission station at Ch'ai Pu. When the evangelist learned why they came, he pounded on the gong to announce a meeting and the house was soon full of people, for every one loves to see a wedding.

It is not customary to wear mourning when being married, but the bride and the groom both wore white shoes. The two young folk who stood up with them wore white shoes also, for their father had recently died a war victim. There they stood, four pairs of white shoes all in a row! When the ceremony was over, the bridal party all walked home together instead of going in two groups as they had come.

Every one marvelled that Excellent Gem had been married without spending more money—it would have cost him one hundred dollars, at least, for the wedding feast. They said that God had especially helped this boy because he tithed his income.

It has now been one year since the wedding, and there is a meeting each night in this Christian home where the neighbors and friends are welcomed. Together the young couple travel the heavenly road, and with united voices they sing of God's faithfulness.

T HE TEACHER sat on a high stool at his rickety little desk. He fanned himself vigorously, for the day was hot. His slanting eyes roved drowsily about the dim little room where a handful of boys shouted at the tops of their voices the lessons which they were memorizing. Slowly he folded his fan and laid it on the table. Then he lifted the teapot and drank from the spout, not taking the trouble to pour the tea into the bowl which sat on the table.

The hsien sheng proudly looked at his hands. He closely scrutinized the long nails of his index and little fingers to estimate how much they had grown during the last year. With a pleased look and a grunt of satisfaction he carefully pushed back his long sleeves and began to write with a camel's hair brush, leaning over the paper, wholly intent upon his task.

Occasionally a boy stopped his monotonous task long enough to stretch lazily and yawn aloud, or to snap his fingers at the flies buzzing around him. When the teacher had finished his writing, he called a slender, serious-faced lad who stood to his feet and bowed respectfully. The boy laid his book on the desk before the teacher. Then he turned his back to prove that he had learned his lesson well. As he recited in a loud, sing-song voice, his body swayed rhythmically while his queue dangled behind him.

When the lad had finished reciting his lesson, he returned to his seat and practiced adding with the abacus. By the time the lessons were over, the sun was sinking in the west, leaving the sky a blaze of red and golden glory. The boys gathered their books into their arms and started for home. There were no

Rev. Wang Feng Ming

chores awaiting them. Those who read books were in a class too honorable for menial tasks.

Thus the days passed and the autumn festival came. School was dismissed for a holiday, and the boys were free to go where they would, seeing this strange sight and that. The parents were superstitious and most of them worshipped idols. One of the boys, Feng Ming, did not seem to be so fun loving as the others. He was very thoughtful and solemn and often went to the temples to worship. His mother had taught him to raise his hands to Buddha and prostrate himself with his forehead to the ground, then raise his clasped hands again to the god until he had bowed himself before Buddha three times.

Feng Ming's parents had married him to a girl with golden-lily feet whom they had selected for him. He had not desired to have a wife, for he often considered going to the mountains of West China and becoming a hermit. He had spent much time in meditation and wondered if living the life of an ascetic might bring happiness to him. He often thought about the end of the soul and pondered as to what became of one after death.

When young Wang was nineteen, he entered a certain "ism" and worshipped by burning incense. The custom was for one to remain on his knees until the stick of incense was all burned. This helped to turn his cogitations toward the Venerable Father in Heaven, whoever and whatever that Spirit might be. Feng Ming's serious manner marked him as one who disciplined himself and as one who did not care to meddle into the affairs of others.

A bookseller came to the village of the Wang family one bright day in early spring and preached about a God whose name was Jesus. A few stragglers gathered around to hear his strange teaching and to examine the gospels which he was selling. Feng Ming came forward with the others and made his way to the stack of books lying on the wheelbarrow, his frank, receptive face full of interest. He selected a New Testament and began to slowly turn the pages, reading a little here and there. Taking a few cash from his girdle and laying them where the colporteur could see, he walked away with the open book in his hand.

The earth of the little court was hard and packed, and there was no waste shrub or flowering plant growing in it, for Mrs. Wang was a thrifty woman and kept a flock of hens. The chickens did not require much feed, for they ran in and out of the house, picking up the crumbs which the children let fall from their chopsticks. Mrs. Wang and her son's wife always watched carefully when a hen sat on the nest which they had made on the ledge outside a lattice window. As soon as a cackle was heard, one of them hurried out to get the egg, fearing that some neighbor's child might carry it away in his sleeve.

Young Wang loved to squat on the ground in a corner of the bare courtyard and ponder as to what life really was. He wanted to sit alone and did not care to talk much with others lest they disturb his meditations. Despondency hung upon his soul like the clouds of darkest night. He sighed deeply as he watched the cool, silvery moon with the thin, fleecy clouds floating over it, sometimes hiding it from his questioning eyes. He wondered who made it. He could not believe that the sun, the moon, the stars, and all the wonders of creation were the work of P'an Ku as he had been taught.

"Who made man to breathe the breath of life?" he sometimes asked himself. "What happens when the soul leaves the body at death—where does the soul go? Are those who die really born again in another form—as a bird, a creeping thing, an animal, or some living being? Is the theory of soul transmigration true?"

123

The young man was wretched, and he did not know why, but the little book made him feel better as he read. He poured over its pages, hour after hour, until he had read the New Testament through seven or eight times. As he studied it, he began to feel that perhaps here was the answer to some of his questions. He could see that there was a God worthy of his homage, but he did not know how to find Him. His heart cried out with Job: "Oh that I knew where I might find Him! That I might come even to His seat!"

A street chapel was opened in a market town not so many miles from the Wang village. When the young man learned about it, he decided that he would go there to hear the book explained. His heart had been so prepared through his reading that he became a Christian almost immediately after hearing the preaching of the cross of Christ. His soul was filled with peace and rest, and his questions no longer troubled him.

Soon after he started going to the street chapel, Wang Feng Ming began to sing some of the glad songs which he heard the Christians sing. One day as he was going through the big front gate at home, humming a tune which he had just heard, everything seemed new and beautiful. The gnarled date tree in the corner of the yard looked more graceful, and the leaves greener and more glossy than he had ever seen them; the chickens scratching in the court appeared to be transformed from drab-colored, common-place fowls to creatures of exquisite coloring. Even the very dust under his feet was more yellow, and the sky was of brighter hue. God was precious to the young man, and name and reputation were as dross. The relatives could not understand what had happened.

"Why do you want to believe in a foreign doctrine?" they asked him.

It was during the year of 1906 soon after the Boxer uprising. When the neighbors learned that Wang Feng Ming was a Christian, they persecuted him and would have nothing to do with him. It was the beginning of severe criticism and misunderstanding by his family and friends. The new doctrine was not popular, for many had been killed because of their faith.

"There is a man as good as dead," declared the neighbors. "He'll have his head cut off just like those other fools who followed the foreign devils' teaching. He'll be killed for his faith, unless we can persuade him to give up this belief. Just wait, and you'll see!"

But the young man did not turn back. Instead of becoming discouraged, he was more earnest all the time. God gave him courage, and he was not afraid. The devil and persecution did not triumph over him; he overcame every hindrance through the victorious Christ who is always conqueror. He read his Bible every day, no matter how busy, and he took time for prayer.

Mother Wang worshipped many idols. She longed to show her devotion to the gods by giving one of her children to Buddha. She had hoped that her oldest son, Feng Ming, would plan to be a priest, but the father wanted him to stay at home, so engaged him to a country girl.

One day when Mrs. Wang was at the temple, she talked with the nun who slept behind Kwangyin, the Goddess of Mercy. This nun had been very ill when she was a tiny child

125

of four years. No doctor could cure her. When the mother saw that her pretty baby was doomed to die, she carried her to the Buddhist temple. Although the little one was very sick, the gods had willed that she live and serve them all her life. The nuns had cared for her, and her mother had made her a new jacket every year while she was small, but she could never go home again. After she grew up, she helped care for others who were dedicated to the gods. Her head was always shaved, and she wore a cap much like the priests wore.

Now that the children were growing up rapidly, Mother Wang began to give up her secret hope. Since it seemed that she could not offer a child, she must try to show her appreciation to Buddha in some other way. She spent so much time burning incense in her home and talking with the nuns at the temple, that she could think of little else. She was afraid of evil spirits, especially since her son had become a Christian. She was more fervent and devout in her idol worship than ever.

Sometimes a demon took possession of Mrs. Wang, and her husband would use sorcery to drive it out. But there was one time when he could do nothing with the evil spirit. It was in the night, and the son was fast asleep. His father called him. Although he was still just a new Christian, he laid his hands on his mother's head and prayed for her. After he had done this three times, the demon left, never to return. No longer did the parents hinder their son. Moreover, they became less zealous about idol worship. In fact, they were almost indifferent.

The young Christian felt stupid and unworthy of being God's child, but there was no wavering or doubting in his heart. He wished to respect his parents, but he could not follow their heathen customs. However, he consulted with his parents when a missionary invited him to assist in the work at one of the mission stations. He decided that he would shine for the Lord and that he would take his stand for the gospel of Jesus Christ. Just two years after his conversion, he became an evangelist to his own people.

During the first years of his ministry, the young preacher sold gospels and witnessed at the markets and fairs. He assisted the missionaries when they opened the work in the walled city of Tungchangfu. That first year Mr. Wang asked that God would give them thirty converts in that new station. Before the year was ended, there were forty!

In 1912, after being a Christian for six years, Mr. Wang keenly felt the need of a deeper experience. He knew that he was God's child, but there was a constant struggle in his heart between the flesh and the Spirit, such as Paul describes in Galatians 5:17. Like John Wesley, he felt that through faith he could be cleansed from all sin, for he read in Matthew 5:8, "Blessed are the pure in heart, for they shall see God." Surely there must be such an experience for him or the Bible would not have suggested it. He sought with full purpose of heart, for he felt that he could never see God unless his heart was made pure. For two weeks he prayed earnestly and searched God's Word. In I John 1:7, he read: "But if we walk in the light, as He is in the light, we have fellowship one with another, and the blood of Jesus Christ His Son cleanseth us from all sin."

Mr. Wang felt that he was walking in all the light that he

had received. Therefore the cleansing from all sin was his heritage; it was his to appropriate. Kneeling in utter abandonment, he consecrated himself anew to God. Great peace filled his soul, and a deep welling up of joy possessed him. God's Son had cleansed him from all sin! New power was given him for service. It was his to keep walking in the light and yielding entirely to God's will, moment by moment, to keep this glorious experience.

Not long after that Mr. Wang helped start the work at Shallow Mouth Town, only six miles from Nankwantao. In a short time, seventy or eighty were attending the meetings. During that year, over two hundred adults took their stand for Christ, besides a number of children.

"My home is happy and cheerful," testified Mr. Wang a few years ago. "I have six girls and one boy. My oldest daughter is married. The second one, Esther, teaches in an elementary school. She is a good Christian, and every one admires her character. She is like salt and light in her influence for good (Matthew 5). She wanted to enter the Tientsin Seminary, but has not yet had the opportunity. The younger children are in school. The promise to my house is that our needs shall be supplied. Although I am but an earthen vessel, the Spirit deigns to dwell within. I want to testify for Him. I expect to serve God all my life. I will work for Him whether I receive wages or not; no matter what persecution or privation I must endure, still I will preach the gospel."

The oldest daughter taught school for a time and then studied nursing at Dr. Mary Stone's hospital in Shanghai. A few years later, she married a Christian official, but he did not live long after that. The young widow is now a nurse in a hospital in West China. She has a darling little son, Moses, who is nearly old enough to go to school.

Esther is now the wife of a Christian leader who serves under Chiang K'ai Shek. The son has graduated from high school and hoped to enter the Tientsin Seminary last fall. He wants to prepare himself for work in the great harvest field of China. The younger children are now deprived of school privileges since the country is in such a disturbed state.

Mr. Wang worked at Fangerchai, one of our important outstations at the beginning of the war. About that time, a large robber band spread through that part of the country. The Christians met together to fast and pray. There seemed to be an invisible wall about them. The robbers did not come to the town, although they were very near.

The Christians of Fangerchai were very zealous to go out and witness on Sunday afternoons. There were twelve gospel teams which went to different villages. Some of the volunteers also gave much time to helping at the markets and fairs. One earnest Christian had to stay at home to feed his ox, or else remain away for only part of the day. He sold the ox rather than let it hinder him. This Christian often gets up in the night to talk to God.

The guerrillas drove the people of Fangerchai from their homes and filled the wells with dirt, so that the Japanese could not live in the town with most of the people gone and the water supply so limited. The Wangs stayed on at the mission and used water from a filthy pond. The people took their belongings with them when they left town, but many of them returned to smoking ruins where their homes had once been.

Soldiers have looted the mission station three times, taking things from the refugees and the workers. These times of danger have only driven the people to see that God is the only one who can help them. During three months of suffering and heartbreak, nine families burned their idols and turned to the true God.

Wang Feng Ming graduated in the first class of our Shantung Training School. Afterward, he assisted in teaching other workers, particularly volunteers. Through the years, Mr. Wang has been a thorough student of the Bible and a capable teacher and preacher. Each message shows that he has spent time in its preparation. Mr. Wang was ordained with our first group of pastors. The Chinese, as well as the missionaries, have found that they are conferring with one who has sound judgment when they go to Pastor Wang for counsel.

Pastor Wang had been stationed at Kuanhsien a few months before Japan declared war on the United States. December eight he was arrested and taken to jail. When he was released, he found that thieves had stolen all of his grain, as there was no one to watch the mission station. Only the clothing which he had on was left him, and he had very little money.

Pastor Wang had arranged with Pastor Chang at Nankwantao to visit a number of the outstations in the Nankwantao district. They wanted to encourage the Christians to do their utmost in supporting the workers, since all funds from America had been cut off. Pastor Wang was at Nankwantao, ready to start on this mission the very day that Pastor Chang laid down his life. Mr. Wang went back to his own station, but he, too, seemed to be in danger so went to another village. It has not seemed wise for him to live at Kwanhsien since, so he goes from station to station, a few days in each place, holding revival meetings and helping the Christians in their problems.

A missionary once heard Pastor Wang use this illustration in a sermon: "We are like the ox. What does it do? It works all of its life and, at last, it is butchered for food."

Pastor Wang says that God has given him a new vision within the last months, and that eternal values have a greater place in his life. His burdens are heavy. He has grown much older during the trying days of war and unrest. He says that he wants God to make him a good shepherd of the sheep. He is determined to bear the cross of Christ to the very end.

"Not for ease or worldly pleasure,
Nor for fame my prayer shall be;
Gladly will I toil and suffer,
Only let me walk with Thee."

FAITHFUL UNTO DEATH

THE CHUBBY, rosy-cheeked little fellow, clumsy in his padded, seatless trousers, was as dear to the hearts of his parents and grandparents as a costly pearl. To make any evil spirit or god who might wish to harm him believe that he was a girl and unworthy of their notice, his mother had him wear a ring in his left ear.

The first time his mother took him with her to a temple, he was afraid when he saw the big stone lions guarding the entrance to the yard. He began to whimper and would go no farther until she took him by the hand and coaxed him past the terrible-looking monsters.

He feared the cruel-faced gods inside the temple. When his mother pointed out a goddess of more genial face, who protected children in danger and kept them from illness, he quickly prostrated himself before her. His mother knelt beside him on the earthen floor, mumbling a few words of thanksgiving. She implored the goddess to keep her child from harm through another year. They left some incense smoldering before the idol when they quietly withdrew from the corner where she sat.

From early childhood, K'un Shan was more dependable and honest than most Chinese boys. One day when his mother began to scold her eldest son's wife because she found a broken teapot lying on the table in the kitchen, the lad returned from his play in the street in time to hear the abusive language. He interrupted quickly. "Mother, my eldest brother's wife did not do it! I struck the teapot against the corner of the table when I was pouring a drink for myself."

The mother was silent.

If the boy made a promise of any kind, he always kept it, even though his playmates sometimes laughed at him because he did not resort to falsehood to save himself from embarrassment. Of course, his elders loved him so much that they seldom did more than scold him mildly if he were naughty. They usually threatened to punish him severely the next time, although they knew that he had been up to some mischievous prank.

K'un Shan had been taught filial obedience, and he had great respect for his elders. If the kindly-faced, white-bearded grandfather asked the boy to accompany him on a visit to a shrine or a temple he always went. Sometimes this meant to give up his plan of going out with the other boys to fly his kite, or of trying to catch the red-breasted bird which he had seen the day before and wanted to put in a cage.

One bright afternoon in the late spring when the days were beginning to grow hot, the grandfather took the lad with him to a famous temple a few li from the town. The eleven-year-old lad thoughtfully slowed his step to the leisurely gait of the aged man. They followed the dusty, winding footpaths through the fields of growing grain. Before them they could see the green-tiled, great sloping roofs of the picturesque buildings shining in the sun above the tree tops. There was a graceful pagoda a short distance from the temple buildings. A well-worn path connected the two interesting places. Large locust trees were in full bloom, filling the air with their pleasant fragrance. The boy wanted to sit under the trees and breathe deeply of their sweetness, but the grandfather declared that they must first perform their duty inside.

Together the tottering old man and the grandson entered the cool, shady building. Its great red pillars reached to the high ceiling where pigeons cooed softly as they roosted on the beautifully carved rafters. Some of the gilded gods wore dust covered, richly embroidered, flowing robes, and their gaudy headdress was adorned with bright beads and long silken tassels.

There were small tables, covered with squares of unhemmed red cloth, before a few of the idols. Untidy little pots of incense ash sat on the tables. The grandfather took some joss sticks from a little bundle which he carried in his hand. He lighted one or two before each of the more important-looking gods.

When they had finished their worship in the temple, they walked outside and sat down on the ground to rest. Bees hummed soothingly while they gathered honey from the locust blossoms. The pagoda bells tinkled softly as they swayed in the gentle breeze. The sound of children's voices could be heard in a near-by village, and the rumble of two-wheeled carts as they jolted along a big road in the distance. The boy lay on the ground, pillowing his head on a brick. Soon he was fast asleep. The grandfather also yielded to drowsiness. Leaning his back against a big tree with his toothless mouth standing ajar he was soon snoring noisily.

Only a few people visited the temple that day. They did not disturb the two who were sleeping so soundly. Presently a wheelbarrow came along the narrow path which cut across one corner of the yard. As it came near the trees, it stopped. The sudden ceasing of the squeaking noise aroused Grand-

Mrs. Chang K'un Shan

father Chang. Slowly he arose and looked about him, yawning aloud and scratching his shaven head. When he saw the two men were looking at him, he took his small black satin cap from the ground and put it on his head. Smoothing the wrinkles from his long gown, he sauntered toward them.

One man, bare to the waist, pushed the wheelbarrow on

which there was a large black box fastened with a crude brass padlock. Besides the box there were several packages. The other man had the manner of a teacher, and he called to Grandfather Chang, "We borrow light, Venerable Gentleman! May I trouble you to tell me if this small road leads to Ch'eng An?"

"Aye, it does, sir. My grandson and I must be returning to the city ourselves before the big gates are closed for the night. We may as well go a little early. I will awaken the boy, and we will go with you. Will you not rest here a few moments before you go on?"

"You very much waste your heart, Old Gentleman. May I ask your honorable name?"

The boy sat up and rubbed his eyes. Then he yawned loudly and stretched himself lazily before he stood to his feet. He heard the stranger say that his name was Miao, and the man asked Grandfather Chang, as courtesy demanded, how old he was. The old man humbly replied that his years had been few and useless—he would be sixty-five quite soon.

As they walked together behind the wheelbarrow, the grandfather politely inquired of Mr. Miao what his business was at Ch'eng An. Mr. Miao said that he had come from a mission station in South Chihli (now Hopei) Province and that he expected to sell books and teach the Jesus religion. He hoped to rent a chapel where he could prepare living quarters in the back. For the present he planned to live at an inn until he could find a suitable place.

Mr. Chang had not heard the new teaching himself. Some of his friends who had heard declared that it was a good doc trine. Grandfather Chang knew of a building that could be rented. He began to plan secretly how he could handle the money so that a little of the silver might stick to his own palm in the passing. He offered to take Mr. Miao by the place. It was just what he wanted. Mr. Chang advised the evangelist not to see the landlord himself, but to trust the entire matter to him. Mr. Chang asked for more money than the owner of the property had agreed upon because he felt that he should have something for his trouble. The next day, the old man carefully struck each dollar against another to see that the silver was sound. Then he gave the lease to Mr. Miao and carried the money to the landlord.

The evangelist hired masons to put a partition in the room so that he could have an inner place for his living quarters. The inside was white-washed, and the outside was plastered with fresh mud. A carpenter made backless benches from a big log which first was sawed into thick slabs. When the red paint had dried on the benches and the window frames, Mr. Miao bought a small laquered table and a stiff black chair to match. He pasted clean white paper on the inside of the window looking upon the street and some pictures and gospel texts on the wall. Then he wrote on a smooth board in large characters, Fu Yin T'ang, "Gospel Hall." He hung the board beside the door where all who passed could see what the place was.

When all was ready, Mr. Miao called at the home of the Changs to invite them to come to the gospel hall. While they sipped tea together he told them something about the doctrine which he had come to teach. Grandfather Chang promised that he would take his grandson to the preaching hall that very night. Just to be gracious, the boy's father and older brother promised that they would be there also, but they had no intention of going.

Children are always ready for anything new or curious, so quite a number of K'un Shan's little friends were at the service. They learned a simple chorus that first evening and enjoyed looking at a large picture while Mr. Miao explained the meaning of it to them. They memorized a verse of Scripture, too.

The boy's first impression of Jesus was that He was just another god, but better and more powerful than the ordinary ones. He seldom missed a meeting during the next three years, but his grandfather rarely accompanied him. His parents, being so bound to their gods that they were loathe to give them up, had nothing to do with the Jesus place.

K'un Shan grew quite fond of the pleasant-faced evangelist who taught him a great deal. When he wanted to become a Christian, about the time he was fourteen, his parents did not object. The truth was, they approved. They had heard some say that the church was powerful and could help people when they had lawsuits. They had known people to come out ahead because the priest used his influence for them when they were having a trial at court. The Jesus people could probably give their converts the same assistance if they were in need of it. The boy's family could see that he promised to become a man of influence. With the prestige of the mission back of him, they thought that he would be able to manage any one in the village who tried to take advantage of the family.

It was a happy occasion for K'un Shan when Mr. Miao took

him to the mission school at Tamingfu in 1921. Some one preached on "The Rich Man and Lazarus" soon after he began his studies, and his heart was greatly moved. He had been sure that there was one true God, and that He was the one who ruled the world. Now he accepted Jesus as his own Savior. He felt impressed that God had chosen him for some special purpose, and he testified many years later that from

Chang K'un Shan at His Ordination Service

the time of his conversion he never turned away from the Lord, although there were times when his love was not as warm as it should have been.

K'un Shan's parents let him go to school. They hoped, however, that he would get homesick and come back to them, for they saw that he had ability to get things done. They felt that it would be better for him to be married, settle down, and help work the land.

They had spoken to a few close friends asking them to

search for an attractive girl. They did not desire a maid from a home of great prosperity lest she not know how to work and manage economically. Neither did they want one whose family was too poor to keep their daughter and her offspring supplied with cloth for their clothing, as was the custom in that part of the country. They looked here and there for a suitable maiden. When they told the boy of their good intentions, thinking that he would want to come home to stay if they had a wife for him, he was much displeased about the whole thing.

"If you engage me to a heathen girl," K'un Shan announced to his mother, "I will go far from home. It will be the same as though you had no second son, for I shall not return."

When the parents saw that the boy meant what he said, they thought it best to let the matter rest for the present.

K'un Shan got along well with his schoolmates. He was not given to quarrelsomeness or boastfulness, for there was an excellent spirit in him. His conduct and straightforward manner won the hearts of all his teachers. When he graduated from the common school at the age of nineteen, the other teachers requested that he be asked to teach in the primary department.

The teachers in the girls' school were concerned because there was a promising girl in the school who had reached the advanced age of twenty and was not even engaged! She should have been married three or four years ago, but her parents were determined that she must have a Christian husband or none at all. A few years ago her home was one of heathen darkness, where gods of paper and wood were worshipped. As she listened to a missionary, her heart was strangely stirred. Her parents had also listened. They did not oppose the thirteen-year-old girl when she accepted Christ as her personal Savior. Soon after that the parents turned to the Lord also, and the home was changed.

When those who would act as go-betweens for the young lady found that K'un Shan was not engaged, they felt sure that it was God's will for him to betroth the girl. The young man considered himself very fortunate to find a Christian girl who would have as much schooling as he had if she finished two more years, and she was only one year older than he. Without waiting to consult his parents, he became engaged to her.

The parents were very unhappy when they learned that their son was engaged to a Christian girl. They were hurt because he had not shown them the respect due them. It was their duty to choose his wife, and he had not even asked their advice in the matter! The mother thought that it would be humiliating to have a daughter-in-law with such big feet. She did not want the neighbors to know that her baby boy had been so inconsiderate and unfilial, but she worried every day and talked to her own family about it.

"I suppose that she will not want to stay at home and work as a wife should. She will probably want to go to the mission, running to and fro on the street just like a harlot!" fretted Mrs. Chang.

"Students know nothing of work," agreed the older son's wife.

"And what will she know of the 'Three Obediences?' I'll swear that if she had been obedient to her elders she would have been married and had children before now!" exclaimed Mrs. Chang in disgust. "How can one expect her husband to be able to control her, or that she will listen to her sons in her old age? She may not even have any sons. Whoever thought that my baby would bring such grief to us? Ai-ya! Ai-ya! (Alas! Alas!)"

When the young man was twenty-one he married and took his bride home for the first time at the New Year. Although he had carried water and swept the courtyard when he was at home for vacations, his family knew that this was unusual for a boy who had read books. They felt sure that his wife would be unwilling to endure the hardships of a poor home and that she would have a different attitude toward things. Knowing their opinion of her, the little bride did everything possible to show them that an educated girl could work and that she was willing to serve her mother-in-law.

The girl helped with whatever there was to do in the home. One day the mother-in-law prepared to make raised white bread with thick-skinned dates in it. K'un Shan knew that his mother was planning to offer this steamed bread to the idols. "Mother, we will obey you in what you ask us to do," he said in a firm, quiet voice, "only this one thing my wife must not do."

"All right, if he will not let you do it, then I can get along without your help. You can feed the fire under the kettle for me, though, and work the bellows to make the fire hotter."

The man looked sadly at his mother and wondered why she would still cling to her gods. He said, "No, mother. She cannot feed a fire for the gods, either."

142

The walls and ceiling of the rooms had been swept and fresh paper put on the windows. Bright red papers with fitting characters written on them were pasted on the doors. Opposite the doorways were long strips of new red paper with the four characters, K'ai men chien hsi, or "Open the door and see happiness."

For a few days the mother and the older son's wife had been busy grinding grain for flour, chopping meat and vegetables for the little meat balls, and making sweet cakes. These had been put aside to wait for the joyful day to come. The last things to be done were now being finished.

In the early morning hours, everyone arose, excepting the young man and his wife. They waited until the idol worship was finished in the home and the members of the family had gone to the temples by the light of a flickering lantern and returned. Then they arose and kowtowed to the grandparents, the parents and the older brother and his wife.

Some of the meat dumplings were cooked in the night, and everyone ate all that he could hold. During the first hours of the morning a new kitchen god was pasted to the wall. The other gods had been torn down and fresh ones put up in their places.

K'un Shan went back to bed to wait for the day to break. When it was light he took some of the steamed bread and went out to preach. There were many visitors that day, and the father and older son went out to make calls on their friends and relatives. The grandfather was not able to get about much those days so stayed with the women.

Tea was poured and some kind of food served to the many

who called to express their congratulations and extend good wishes for the coming year. In a few days, before the end of the holidays, the Red Spears arose in rebellion. The young couple hurried to get away before the roads were impassible.

Some years before when Grandfather Chang's strength began to fail, his son decided that it was time to buy a coffin for him. The head man at the carpenter shop offered to reduce his prices considerably if Mr. Chang would purchase two coffins at the same time. Knowing that sooner or later his mother would need one also, the man took advantage of the bargain and made provision for both of his parents at the same time.

The huge coffins, one stacked on top of the other to save space, were crowded into the room close by the k'ang, where the old folks could see them the first thing every morning as soon as they opened their eyes. They were greatly comforted as they felt of the hard wood and noted its thickness. They commended their son for his thoughtfulness and for his shrewdness at bargaining.

Just before dawn one morning in the early autumn, the grandfather suddenly died. A messenger hurried to call K'un Shan. While they were waiting for him to come, they tore down the red papers from the doors and put up white ones to show that death had come.

When the grandson arrived, he greeted the members of the family. Then he lifted up his voice and wept. And while he mourned, the others wept also, so that the lamenting could be heard quite a distance from the courtyard. When they grew calm again they told K'un Shan that he was to take charge of the funeral arrangements. Although he was younger than the others, no one else in the family had much courage or skill in dealing with men, and there would be much to do in arranging for the feast and engaging pall-bearers and grave diggers. Since he had some education and was highly respected by all the townfolk, there was no question about his being the one to manage the affairs.

The grandson consented to do his best if they would agree to what he had to say. It was this: "We will not shao (burn incense at the home, and paper money and other articles at the grave). We will not liao (put offerings before the spirits and gods). We will not pao (announce to the gods in the temple)."

When he saw by the faces of some of the relatives that they were not pleased with what he said, he told them that he would return to the school immediately if they wanted a heathen funeral. They were afraid that there was no one else who could assume such great responsibility if K'un Shan left. But they considered it very important to have a great display for one who was so old when he died. They felt angry to think that there would be no paper horses and carts, or palaces and slaves burned at the grave. To them it did not seem honorable for one of such great age to be buried so simply. They were humiliated that no more money was to be spent.

An aunt had declared that the simplicity of the funeral was all because K'un Shan was so stingy. She decided to go to the home at the next New Year and see if there were any new idols in the home. If there were, then she would know that it was just the young man's stinginess. But if there were no gods, then she would believe that he was really a Christian. This time, when the young couple went home for the vacation, he removed every idol. His parents did not approve. They were afraid that some evil might befall them, but they did not dare stop him. The aunt looked here and there. When she saw that there were no images in the home, her anger went out of her.

After teaching for a few years Mr. Chang took some training class work and then went to an outstation to do evangelistic work. Their first child, a son, was named Lu En, which means Shantung Grace because he was born soon after they came to Shantung. When the Tientsin Bible Seminary opened, Mr. Chang enrolled in the first class. His wife continued to work as a Bible Woman. Each summer he went back to work with her for three months.

There were times during those school days when there was no money and no food in the house. They sometimes ate wild greens and flowers and young leaves and buds from the poplar trees. Once when they sorely needed new clothing and there was no money, Mr. Chang wrote to his home and asked his folk to send them some of the cotton which they had produced on their land. But they would not, even though he had sent home most of his salary when he was teaching school.

During the three years that Mr. Chang was in the school he was a real leader. He preached at different places in the city of Tientsin, one of them being an independent tabernacle supported and managed entirely by the Chinese. They considered Mr. Chang a strong preacher with vitality in his messages, and they had been having noted preachers from many parts of China who had given them strong meat.

Mr. Chang also superintended a Sunday School of children in his practical work. It was at a village across the river from the school. The children were so wild that it was hard to do anything with them, but they calmed down under the careful and prayerful supervision of their leader. Some of them were converted. When a table was needed for the room and there was none, Mr. Chang went through the streets of the city, carrying a table on his back for the three li.

Let us read part of Chang K'un Shan's own testimony as he wrote it out before his graduation: "I want to praise the Lord because He removed all hindrances to my entering the Seminary. The spiritual benefits I have received here are beyond description. I would like to mention all of them, but can only speak of a few. My faith has been strengthened; I have received much instruction from the Bible; I have closer fellowship with my Lord than formerly; my strength to labor for Him has been increased. The purpose of my life may be found in Acts 6:4, 'But we will give ourselves continually to prayer, and to the ministry of the word.' Wherever the Lord leads me I will follow, no matter what the conditions may be—whether the way is bitter or sweet. I am determined to follow. My prayer is that men may be saved, and this is the aim of my life."

After finishing his course at the Seminary, Mr. Chang was stationed at Nankwantao, where he labored for seven years. He rode his bicycle out to different villages where he had meetings in the homes. He gave much time to revival meetings at other stations, not only in the Nankwantao district, but throughout the whole field.

When the workers came in from the twenty outstations of the district with their problems, Mr. Chang was always ready to give a sympathetic ear to them and help bear their burdens in any way that he could. After ministering to the people of Nankwantao for four years, they volunteered to take the support of both Mr. and Mrs. Chang. In May, 1941, Mr. Chang was ordained to be a pastor.

Mr. Chang was a man of prayer. When the Changs were stationed at Nankwantao, a government school teacher gave them a parting gift as they were ready to leave the outstation where they had been working. This teacher was hungry-hearted, for she had been in the same school with Mrs. Chang. She had once known what it was to have peace in her heart. But she had traveled the road of sin and saw no way to be free from the fetters that bound her. In thanking her for the vegetables, Mr. Chang said, "In return for your kindness, we will take the responsibility upon our own hearts of praying for your salvation. Do not feel that there is no hope for you."

In a public service, Mr. Chang told us that God could save any one and that he had prayed for three persons until their lives had been changed. One was the teacher. Another said that he would repent if the sun would rise in the west once. The third one said that he would believe that there was a God in heaven if he could see a stone fall from the skies and kill a child or two. Hard cases? Yes. How did God work for them? Mr. Chang told us: "The first one is all for Jesus now, and she is here today. The second one is in school preparing to enter the ministry. The third one is now preaching the gospel."

When robbers came to the town and nearly every one fled the Changs stayed at their post. When war came with refugees flooding the mission compound, they let the distressed people pile bundles and boxes in their home as high as the ceiling. They were so crowded that they had to circle around the things whenever they entered the room.

Mr. Chang took a special interest in the government school teachers who also found refuge at the mission. His joy was complete when five of them turned to the Lord. He also prayed with a number of prominent men of the town and rejoiced with them when the burden of sin rolled from their hearts.

Pastor Chang was very fond of children, having six of his own. Four girls were born after Shantung Grace. The parents named them Glorious Grace, Beautiful Grace, Abundant Grace and Guiding Grace. Each evening there was a meeting at the Chang home for all the children in the compound. Some of the children who attended the meetings at the outstation six years ago still talk of the stories they heard then. They can never forget the impression made on their minds when Mr. Chang told them about the little Syrian maid.

January 26, 1942 the children of the workers all gathered at the Changs as usual. Two girls who had been attending a mission high school until Japan declared war on America had returned to their homes at the mission station at Nankwantao. They had learned some new songs while away, and they taught one of them to Pastor Chang that night. He liked

149

it so much that he sang it until nearly midnight, "Lord, I Will Carry the Cross."

A letter arrived from Mr. Chang at that time and this is what it said: "There are two songs in my heart as I think of my work: 'Where He Leads Me I Will Follow,' and 'Jesus Is Dearer Than All.' God has helped us here because you friends there have been praying for us. The official here gave me twenty dollars to help pay for my office things—everything is gone! I had to hunt to find this scrap of paper on which to write you, and it is not very respectable. I use a lead pencil because I have no pens left. Very little has been returned— a small amount of medicine and a few empty bottles from the dispensary things. Please do not be anxious about us, but do pray much for our future. Emanuel."

Tuesday morning, January 27, Pastor Chang spent some time with his Bible and in communion with his Lord. When he came from the place of prayer, he washed and was just ready to eat his breakfast. A soldier arrived from the Japanese headquarters saying that Pastor Chang, Mr. Wang, who was chairman of the Nankwantao district, and Mr. Cheng, who had charge of the dispensary work, were wanted immediately. The men had been trying to get back more of the things which the Japanese had seized when they took possession of the mission property December 8, and they thought that perhaps they were being called for this purpose.

When they reached the official's place, they were told that they must wait to see him as he was still busy. But the men were somewhat troubled when Pastor Chang was asked to go to one room, and they were led to another. In a very

150

short time a Chinese interpreter told the two men that Pastor Chang was to be killed, as they had found him guilty of giving information to the Chinese Communists. Pastor Chang had ridden out to some villages on his wheel, where he had meetings with the Christians. The Japanese suffered heavy losses in a battle six or seven miles away the day before. Although there was no trial, Pastor Chang was accused of warning the Chinese guerrillas that there was to be a battle.

Although both men fell on their faces and begged that the life of their co-worker be spared, it was useless. They were ordered to go back to the mission and send men to carry the body away for burial. They were commanded to leave the mission compound immediately, but they pleaded for permission to stay one day longer. They could hardly finish moving in one day, since they did not know where they could go. They were told that they might have until the next day to vacate the premises.

The men went home and told their wives what had happened, and they sent men to bring the corpse home. Mr. Wang took Mrs. Chang with him to select a coffin.

Just as the body was being carried into the mission yard, Mrs. Chang's aged father arrived bringing her some grain. He knew that the support which the Changs received was not sufficient to feed so many mouths, even though Lu En was being supported in the mission school where his father had been a teacher.

There was no time for a real funeral. The faithful worker still wore his blood-stained garments when they placed him in the rough coffin. A prayer was offered, and the men laid brick around and over the huge box, using mud for mortar. Pastor Chang's face wore the usual smile, but there was a tiny hole under one eye where a bullet had come through, and a larger one where the cruel lead had entered the back of his head.

The workers moved out, finding places wherever they could. Mrs. Chang went to her father's home for a short time, but she lived in a rented house at Nankwantao until her father could return to his home and bring a wheelbarrow for her babies. There were many people who longed to give Mrs. Chang a home with them at the time, but their hearts were so filled with fear over what had happened that they did not dare to go near her. Two Christian men walked in from their country homes and looked for Mrs. Chang until they found where she lived. They gave her some money. They wept aloud as they walked by the mission compound where God had spoken peace to their hearts.

Soon after her sorrow, Mrs. Chang wrote us and sent the letter by a woman who was coming to Tungchangfu to attend her mother's funeral. The woman came to my room one night. She untied the band around one trouser leg and carefully pulled a tightly folded piece of thin paper from the wadding in her garment. This is what the Chinese characters said:

"Precious Seal, my sister, peace to you. Thank God that in this time of trouble He especially gives me peace because His will has been done in the body of Shantung Grace's father. God saw that his burdens were too heavy. That day, on December 8, the Lord said to me, 'His work is done.'

"I saw his face after they brought him home, and it looked very nice, no change at all. He looked better than I ever saw him, therefore, my heart is at peace, but in the flesh we can but be sad. I feel that we in the Lord should be glad that his labor is ended and that now he enjoys eternal bliss and happiness. Oh, that I might leave this world of suffering immediately! Truly, it is bitter.

"I plan to go to my father's home and then come back and stay with Mrs. Jen at East Su Ts'un. God has spoken to me, and I cannot disobey. Riches or poverty, I will follow Him all the way. 'Where He Leads Me' and 'All to Jesus I surrender' are my songs these days. If the Lord reduces me so that I must beg, I will still work for Him. I have no other purpose. Are you all right? I am so melancholy."

Excerpts from Mrs. Chang's second letter:

"I truly believe that God will not let me have difficulty above that I can bear. He knew that I could endure this or He would not have permitted me to meet it. He knew that I could stand all that He has put upon me. Unworthy as I am, He wants me to la t'ao (stretch the tugs as an ox pulling a load) for Him. God early revealed to me that I must pass through a great trial—but who would have thought it would be this?

"Pai Wen Cheng (a faithful Christian man who lives in the town) carries water for me. My circumstances are something like Jesus met when He was before the Sanhedrin, but God has not forsaken me. Therefore rest your heart about me, for I will not listen to the devil.

"I have read Ecclesiastes three times since my great sorrow, and I have received much teaching from it."

When Mrs. Chang learned that we must leave China she wrote:

"I am so sad that you may have to leave. If you can, send me a letter and tell me why. Only God can be depended upon. Vain is the help of man, but God will not cast me off. I have received so much help from First Peter these days.

"I know that you constantly pray for me, and I do not forget to pray for you. I am now with Mrs. Jen and I am happy here. We go out together nearly every day to visit the Christians, and we have

Sunday meetings in her courtyard. Every night a number of the people of this village meet together, and the Christians come here from other villages on Thursday afternoon for the prayer meeting.

"I have Glorious Grace and baby (a little boy about one year old) with me, and the other children are with my mother. Glorious Grace looks after the baby so that I am free for the work of the Lord."

When Mrs. Chang was requested to write me something of her husband's life she wrote the following:

"The father of my children traveled the way of the cross. His conscience was void of offense towards God and men. No matter what came, he wanted to go on, living a life of faith, suffering hardship for the work of the Lord. Many times he was so busy that he could not eat.

"He was patient and not one to criticize others. He did not discuss the weak or the strong points of his friends. He did not want to speak idle words, but wanted everything he did to count for the Lord.

"During the seven years that he worked at Nankwantao, he had no misunderstanding which led him to break fellowship with a fellow worker or any of his sheep. He did rebuke some who needed it, for he felt that he would not be a faithful shepherd unless he did this. He rebuked, exhorted, and warned. He did not seek the good will of folk at the expense of the work, but he dared to be true to them. He was a real worker and led many souls to God. He did not know that his days were numbered and that his course would soon be run.

"He arose early and went to bed late. Every morning he took time to be alone with his Bible and his God. Every day we had prayers in the home. Each evening all the children in the yard were invited to come to our home for singing and memory work, a Bible story and prayer.

"Evil-doers called him before he had breakfast, and he had been too busy to eat the night before. His face was shining, and he looked so happy as he started off that I was just ready to ask him why, but did not.

"In one hour he was carried back to me. He had been singing half the night the evening before and his face still looked happy—it had not changed at all. He was thirty-five years old."

Lu En was fourteen years old (by Chinese count which always makes one a year or two older than our way of reckoning) when his father went to heaven. He has testified in the public services and lived an exemplary life before the other children. This little boy has often said that he wanted to be a preacher when he grew up and eat bitterness like his father.

Yes, Pastor Chang wears a martyr's crown, and he rests from his labors. His wife labors on, winning souls and providing for six little ones. Her father would gladly care for all of them, but he is a poor man. He must produce the food with his own labor, for he has no son to help him. Is he sorry he insisted that his daughter marry a Christian? No, his eyes are looking beyond the present world.

Some day we hope that a memorial service can be held for Pastor Chang in the church at Nankwantao where he preached so often and that a fitting marker can be placed at his grave to remind others that he gave his life for the Lord. Though dead, his messages live today in the hearts of the people.

> "Now the laborer's task is o'er;
>   Now the battle day is past;
> Now upon the farther shore
>   Lands the voyager at last.
> Father, in Thy gracious keeping
>   Leave we now Thy servant sleeping.

> "There the tears of earth are dried;
>   There its hidden things are clear;
> There the work of life is tried
>   By a juster judge than here.
> Father, in Thy gracious keeping
>   Leave we now Thy servant sleeping.

155

" 'Earth to earth, and dust to dust,'
  Calmly now the words we say;
Left behind, we wait in trust
  For the resurrection day.
Father, in Thy gracious keeping
  Leave we now Thy servant sleeping."